Erotic Faculties

University of California Press
Berkeley
Los Angeles
London

Erotic Faculties

JOANNA FRUEH

University of California Press
Berkeley and Los Angeles, California

University of California Press, Ltd.
London, England

Etymologies and definitions are taken from *Webster's New World Dictionary*, 3d College ed., except for those in "Mouth Piece," which are from *Webster's Third New International Dictionary.*

Library of Congress Cataloging-in-Publication Data

Frueh, Joanna.
Erotic Faculties / Joanna Frueh.
p. cm.
Includes bibliographical references and index.
ISBN 0-520-20081-0 (alk. paper).—ISBN 0-520-20082-9 (pbk. : alk. paper)
1. Erotica. 2. Feminism and the arts. 3. Performance art.
I. Title
NX650.E7F78 1996
700—dc20 95-23356

Printed in the United States of America
9 8 7 6 5 4 3 2 1

The paper used in this publication meets the minimum requirements of American National Standard for Information Sciences—Permanence of Paper for Printed Library Materials, ANSI Z39.48-1984.

For Russell

Contents

Acknowledgments

For good or ill, all the people a person has ever met live within her. Some she must exorcise, while she works to increase the presence, if only partial, of others, who have provided comforts and pleasures, opportunities for loving in everyday life and in work. I thank those providers, who have helped me develop and exercise my erotic faculties: you release the perceived taint of the never entirely exorcised; you are the exorcists.

I think of you in the order in which we came into each other's lives.

Erne and Florence Frueh, my parents, whose love has sustained me all my life

Renée Wood, my sister, whose beauties become stronger to me the older we get

Ida and Sam Pass, my mother's parents, who prophesied my future

Sarah Lewis, my oldest friend, a superb and sensuous cook, a delightful traveling companion and drinking partner, who has, for over half our lives, offered her gracious and tranquil self and home whenever I visit New York

Everett Clarke, without whose teachings my voice and spirit would not have thrived as they do

Claire Prussian, with whom I've shared the best of ladies' lunches, the richest talk about fashion, style, cosmetic surgery, the lightness of intimacy

Edith Altman, mystic sister of unquestioning understanding

Arlene Raven, critic comrade of acid and poetic honesty

Carolee Schneemann, courageous erotic

Thomas Kochheiser, who made it possible for me to write about Hannah Wilke, which I had wanted to do for several years, by asking me to write the catalog essay for his Wilke retrospective in 1989

M. M. Lum, whose stories I love

Peggy Doogan, whose trenchant literacy and nasty humor unclog my heart

The students in the first performance art class I taught, at the University of Arizona, in the fall of 1984: David Flynn, Dawn Fryling, Charles Gute, Nancy Hall Brooks, Willie Hulce, Janet Maier, Dan Mejia, Jim Mousigian, Maureen O'Neill, Pat Riley, Susan Ruff
The spell you put on me keeps me charmed

Rachel Rosenthal, so sweet and glamorous

Leila Daw, who shows me the meaning of frenzy, who tells me visions

Kate Rosenbloom, now Anderson, whose laughter and complexion are astonishingly clear

Marla Schor, who gave me a place to live when I had no home

Russell Dudley, whom I married and who married me out of sanity and pleasure, whose acute criticisms are loving touches, whose photographs enrich *Erotic Faculties*

Christine Tamblyn, responsive writing and performing partner

Jeff Weiss, whose lush acerbity and relentless integrity have banished the almost unbearable absurdities of academia and the art world

Helen Jones and Steve Foster, who talk with me about ecstasy, perversions, and ruthless compassion

Members of the Research Advisory Board at the University of Nevada, Reno, who, in 1992, granted me a Faculty Research Award to assist in my research on contemporary women artists and aging, work that informs the chapter in this volume on "Polymorphous Perversities: Female Pleasures and the Postmenopausal Artist"

Johanna Burton and Heidie Giannotti, whose backyard is magic

Naomi Schneider and William Murphy, editor and assistant editor at the University of California Press, whose enthusiasm for the unconventional has made *Erotic Faculties* possible and with whom conversation is erotic

Nola Burger, for the beautiful design of *Erotic Faculties*

Dore Brown and Jane-Ellen Long, at the University of California Press, for their subtle, elegant, and expert treatment of the manuscript

Introduction

I was naked and I remember warmth, which was sunlight and my mother. The sunlight touched my skin, which was a threshold for sensation and love. Love and sensation passed into my organs, tissues, fluids, and into the parts of human being that words as definitions only weakly describe, into my soul, heart, intellect. These loci of liminality defined my bodily existence.

I have no recollection of my contour, the discreteness that turns the human body in the human mind into boundary, barrier, and object. I was lying down, as soft as the sheets or blankets that cushioned me and, like me, radiated light. Perhaps the season was winter and the room well heated. Maybe a summer sun caressed my mother's flesh and mine to whitish gold, and the bedclothes and the air as well.

I was an infant and this is my first memory. I began to think about it a few years ago; I do not recall remembering it before that. Since the memory first returned to me, it has come back often, so that I can know it better. I see now that the primary significance of what I call soul-and-mind-inseparable-from-the-body is rooted in my earliest existence, where eros and psyche were wed.

• • •

Just as human beings have faculties of speech, sight, and hearing, so we have erotic faculties, which are largely underdeveloped. Erotic faculties enable amatory thought, acts, and activism. The erotic thinker and practitioner may focus on sex, but erotic faculties affect all connections that human beings make with other species and with things invisible and visible. Erotic faculties make possible love's arousal and endurance, which can mend false splits within oneself, such as poet and historian or feminist and motherhater, and within communities whose factions, priorities, and hierarchies work against the meaning of community as mutual interest. Love may sound like a simplistic way to alleviate suffering, but the simplicity of love as an answer to despair and to heartless individualism is a complex project for the human spirit. As a person's erotic faculties develop, so does her lust for living.

Mother-child lust, denied within patriarchy's love of man, is a ground from which erotic faculties develop. The erotophobia embedded in the laws and lusts of the fathers is a misunderstanding of the erotic, for an erotic response to life is not specifically genital but, rather, a state of arousal regarding life's richness. Erotic engagement is bodily, psychic, and intellectual, and a mother can, by loving attentiveness, prevail over the erotophobia that a child experiences as socialization and education subdue erotic desire and (work to) tame it out of her, and that a young scholar reads as subtext in book after book. The authority of scholarly standards crushes erotic faculties and their owner, the erotic, who, if she is lucky and determined, and disciplined in her erotic endeavors, will author herself. The author *is* the erotic, who is the only authority on her own erotic faculties, which, allowed to thrive, will overgrow the cloister of scholarly etiquette. Erotic authority loosens scholarly writing and lecturing by changing both the conventional form of an academic paper and accepted scholarly costume and oratory. *Erotic Faculties* makes these changes evident by demonstrating a critical erotics.

The lustful girls and women say
Take me into the bedroom backwards or I will turn you hard
I've got Medusa eyes
If you're as rigid as a rigorous argument
I'll turn you around so hard you may fall down and crumble
I've got erotic eyes
erotic I, she speaks in affirmations

I've got erotic eyes
You haven't lived unless you face us

The standard scholarly voice, of male authority whether used by women or men, has been unitary, flat, dry, and self-censorious. Erotic scholarship is lubricious and undulant, wild, polyvocal, cock- and cuntsure—secure in the erotic potency of bodily particularity unsuppressed by the stereotyped abstractions of age, race, and gender. Cocksure scholarship is not the overbearing sobriety and orderliness of standard academic prose.

To operate as though the human mind speaks to itself and others in only one voice is an ascetic posture. A critical erotics speaks with a sensuous abandonment of intellectual discipline that mortifies the soul-and-mind-inseparable-from-the-body.

An hour before the lecture she was adjusting the sleeves, fitted from shoulder to wrist, of a scarlet dress that bared her knees and shoulders. The light wool jersey skimmed her body. The speaker wore stockings that paled the color of her legs, and black suede slingbacks, with a high heel, that exposed the cleavage of her toes. She examined her face closely, the sparkling gold eyeshadow and black liner, the powder that made the pores on her nose almost invisible and gave her skin a luminous finish. The last touch was lipstick. She outlined her mouth, filled the contours with color that matched her dress, pressed her lips to each other, then to the first page of her lecture.

The rigorous arguments so valued by academics are testimonies to the fact that the thinkers have become stiffs. A rigorous argument may be exact, but the value placed on rigor, the choice of word, indicates the inflexibility of a system that wants to promote itself. Rigor suggests unnecessary austerity, a lifelessness in which the thinker may be in good part dead to the world. In actuality we move through the world and it moves through us. We move each other and are constantly changing. When we're alive to this reality, it moves us, so much that we can't stop moving, and there is no stopping the mind that moves. It is dangerous, and that's a sign of health. The passion of the moving mind sets other minds in motion.[1]

Cock/cunt is moving flesh, full of fluids. To be fluid is to be in love.

I belong to the liquid world of words, I am streaming language, spinning tales, love stories, that go by no single name.

Circum, Latin, around about; *scriba,* Latin, public writer, scribe. I circumscribe myself. I encircle myself with words. I center myself in intersecting spheres of definition, derivation, rhythm, sound, articulation, interpretation.

Centrality is mobile, and circumference is an illusion.

Words have no boundaries. Users manufacture them, control meaning in the making. Conversation, technical jargon, political speeches, and advertising copy simultaneously circumscribe territories and open them up like poetry, which I see as the most indiscrete genre of writing.

Indiscretion counters the "tight-lipped, joyless austerity" that, according to theorist Terry Eagleton, identifies the work of some male intellectuals. The notable virtue of such scholarship is that it is "unsloppy."[2]

Recently I was told by a man who needed to edit an article of mine that it would be tighter without multiple voices. Keepers of scholarly fitness still uphold rigor and tightness. As feminist theorists have pointed out for more than two decades, Western culture has conceptualized woman as the sloppy sex: she bleeds, fluid oozes from her vagina, she produces milk, and her body is softer than man's. *Tight lips don't enjoy the wetness of another mouth, the luscious messiness of saliva.*

Be tight, like a vagina that holds onto a penis solely for a man's pleasure. Like a woman who, lusting for a grip on her own ideas, fears her strangeness once she knows what she wants to know, or tries to conceal herself in man's knowledge, and so grasps the phallus.

Wetness is one signal of a woman's lust. Why should she enjoy making dry arguments? Why should her voice defend the phallus? She questions academics' praise of rigorous analyses. Rigor reminds her not of discipline, which can be lust's focus and satisfaction, but of rigor mortis. She does not want to be an intellectual corpse.

The female body drawn to fit the dimensions of Western art's nude is a diagram of a murder victim. *Victim* derives from the Latin *victima,* victim, beast for sacrifice. Bodily specificity is a key element in the performance of erotic faculties. I picture my body's naked beauty and beastliness whether I am more or less exposed. I offer myself to myself; I accept. I am my own erotic object, to touch and to view, to experience life and to act in it. As long as I am an erotic subject, I am not averse to being an erotic object.

. . .

The erotic scholar is willing to be sloppy, as sex is sloppy—the movements, the fluids people crave and fear in a time of sexual epidemic—as life is sloppy—full of unexpected untidy events jumbled like puzzle pieces in a box. The erotic scholar understands, too, that sex is elegant—the movements, the satisfaction of desire—and that life is also elegant when intellection puts together the pieces of the puzzle.

Discipline, which is any scholar's job, combines sloppiness and elegance into new terms that balance standard academic rhetorical skills and unconventional means of scholarly persuasion. I use exposition and combine it with rhetorical and methodological techniques that do not appear in standard scholarship and that play with words, ideas, and the form of a scholarly paper. *I read a scholar, whose subject was man's loss of virile mission once civilization made unnecessary his hunter role and rituals, who said that playing with language is for children; adults outgrow it. He forgot that play is active pleasure. The erotic scholar would rather pursue a tantalizing idea and incorporate than kill it and turn it into a trophy or some bland food for thought.* Narratives are multiple and fragmented, often told in several literary genres and spoken in various voices, such as seer, lover, psychoanalyst, daughter, manlover, womanlover, friend, elder, prophet, fucker, elegist, singer, bleeding heart, activist, patient, goddess, art critic, mythmaker, and storyteller. Graphic and sexual language are paramount. Other techniques include using personal reflection, parody, autobiography, poems, and lyrical language that could be called poetry. Just as the author's identity shifts in erotic scholarship, so does the reader's, for she cannot expect truth to be served to her declaratively. Standard scholarship inhibits a writer's relationship with an audience in the name of objectivity, transparency, and coherence. But elucidation and evocation are not mutually exclusive; elliptical writing is not superficially visionary or utopian, for it conveys the reality of inconclusiveness; and logical evaluation cannot serve as the only means of interpreting thought. In erotic scholarship, poetry and a kaleidoscopic telling disrupt the asinine explicitness of expository prose.

The writer underwent editing.

She used the term *biologically determined.* The editor, a woman, wrote on the manuscript, "What do you mean by this phrase? *Must* define yourself."

The writer stated that Hannah Wilke "'scars' herself with chewing-gum sculptures. Chewed gum twisted in one gesture into a shape that reads as vulva, womb, and tiny wounds marks her face, back, chest, breasts, and fingernails and marks her, too, with pleasure and pain that are not limited to female experience." The editor exclaimed on the manuscript, "That's a lot for one piece of gum! FIX." The scholar thought, "If it didn't do a lot, it wouldn't be art."

I define myself indefinitely.

Erotic Faculties presents poetry as a foundation for theory, and poetry calls into question exposition's claim to authoritative truthtelling. Feminist poets, critics, and scholars have commented on poetry's ability to incorporate daily life, restructure thought, and move readers and hearers to action. Accordingly, poetry is a necessity for women because it distills their experiences, names them, and turns them into knowledge.[3] Poetry defies transparent meaning with rhythm and patterns of sound, so it exceeds exposition's measured explanations of a subject, which guard the reader against bewilderment.

Be wild, ferocious, lascivious, the teacher thinks as she lectures to her class. She says to them, "Don't worry if you're confused. Confusion doesn't necessarily mean that you don't understand, and what you believe is understanding may have little to do with knowledge. Confusion forces you to think, and the process will lead to clarity—for the moment."

Erotic scholarship owes much to feminism, which inspires the erotic scholar's play, which is pleasure, which delegitimizes convention. *Loose lips sink ships. I author my eroticism, lust for language and images that convey the interplay of psyche and eros.*

Success in scholarship seems to demand conformity. Feminist theorists have written again and again about women's captivity in a language—words, syntax, ideologies, standpoints, rhetoric—invented by men and maintained by male-dominant and masculinist institutions such as the academy. But writing about is not warning against or demonstration of working differently, of writing/thinking/work not as the labor of "*must* define yourself"—always in someone else's terms. Scholarship is then a hardship, a labored love, like working diligently at an intimate relationship, which contemporary American society believes is a necessity. With conformity, an art and act of pleasure—writing—turns, unconsciously, into a way to lose and even hate oneself.

Love That Red, the name, I think, of a lipstick color. Love that red of my own lips, dressed not in metaphors of berries or flowers, but in a blast of color that speaks belief in a vibrant voice. The red mouth has been a metaphor for fruits and female genitals and for women's participation in blood mysteries, but I line and color my mouth to exert the autoerotic faculty of speech.

When I was about twenty-five a friend said to me, "You're autoerotic." I loved her saying that but didn't think that my autoeroticism was particularly unusual. I thought everyone we knew was a practicing autoerotic and that younger generations would follow the autoerotic path. Perhaps the sexual revolution led me to believe this. But the sexual revolution was not an erotic revolution.

I see my women students in their twenties losing their minds and bodies to self-hatred as much as my supposedly or superficially autoerotic generation of women did. My students' self-hatred is not an existential condition of women's youth. Young women's self-doubts and low self-esteem continue because "*must* define yourself" continues, and it extinguishes autoeroticism.

Some feminists' solution to this problem is for women to discover, recognize, and create their own voices. This is exceedingly difficult to do within the proscriptions of academia. Also, women's voices as an oppositional affirmation of otherness, which would celebrate emotion, intuition, delicacy—woman's supposedly natural sensitivities and ways of understanding—is yet another proscription. One of the most important feminist writings on the erotic, Audre Lorde's "Uses of the Erotic: The Erotic as Power," suffers from an assertion of women's sensitivities, which, she says, are naturally invested in the erotic and not the pornographic. Lorde understands that the erotic consists of richness, joy, and profundity in living and that erotic living is socially transformative. That feminists have not developed these ideas of Lorde's as a foundation for a feminist erotics mystifies me. However, for Lorde the erotic signifies tenderness, emotional resonance, and the capacity to love, whereas the pornographic fragments feeling from doing.[4] I cannot distinguish erotic from pornographic. *Words have no boundaries.* Pornography originally meant writing about whores.

whore
ME *hore* < OE < or akin to ON *hora* < IE base *kā-*, to like, be fond of, desire > L *carus,* dear, precious, Latvian *kārs,* lecherous

I desire myself, am the dear one, the pornerotic object for my own delectation, wishing, with lecherous intensity, for the world to be a whorehouse, full of people who define themselves as precious and who know that erotic pleasure need not be delicate.

In your Quest for True Love
You've listened to the lyrics of ten thousand songs
Where words are coupled in
Conventional positions
Like the genders
In the dark
In man's millennia
I've got a mad desire
Look, I'm on fire
With that burning
Undiscerning feeling inside me
Deep inside
My Delta Queen
She was under eighteen
You know what I mean

In your Quest for True Love
You costume me in corsets apricot
And peach, rose and lavender
As if my cunt must be a fruit and flower
Sweetly spiced
I select pearls fresh from my grandma's grave
And silver shoes
In my delirium of living
I do adore myself
As Goddess of the Heart and Hardon
But I am just a beggar

Too bare
For you in simply flesh

How can I repay you for this
Tongue-in-cheek regalia?
For your preservation
Of a few erotic faculties?
For your perseverance in adapting
Any hole to fit your cock?

The next time that I blossom
In your eyes
I will prepare your face
With cherry plum and violet
I will smooth a little color on
Your nipples
I will spray my own cologne
Bellodgia
Fragrant with carnation
Everywhere you'll sweat
When we are fucking
And the next time that you say
    I want to fuck your butt your mouth your cunt
I will jam a dildo up your ass

In your Quest for True Love

A critical erotics puts an end to the scholarly tradition of disembodiment. The erotic scholar's lust for the written intimacy of body and mind exceeds personalization of style and any statement of standpoint: *I am a forty-eight-year-old white woman, a professor of modern and contemporary art, a performance artist, a wife, a baker, a bodybuilder, a manlover, a womanlover, a daughter of Florence and Erne, sister of Renée, a nonpracticing Jew*. Anyone could go on and on trying to make clear from self-identification the embodied circumstances that serve as bases for how and perhaps why she knows what she knows.[5] But embodied scholarship cannot be reduced to what at first seems impossibly complex—all the names one gives oneself. A scholar's concretizing her social location may help the mutual connection between an audience and herself, but erotic scholarship entails speaking from, for, and about the body. The assertion of an "I" requires more than anecdote and autobiography.[6] I base theory on my body and my experiences and on other women's bodies and experiences. No body, no erotic muscle.

Some of the erotic scholar's powers are urgency, immediacy, mobility, and destabilization, which necessitate speech in as many voices as she can or wishes to use. They develop through lust, necessity, and academic and social training, and they allow a scholar to speak in what may seem like contradictions, at least in the realm of scholarly etiquette. Sexual intimacies and intellect, fiction and art history, anecdote and poetry, high emotion and academic restraint, sentiment and historical facts, empathy and objectivity, friends' words from conversations and theorists' words from books all recur in *Erotic Faculties*. Erotic scholarship's grounding in various literary genres produces not closed, seamless arguments but, rather, dances with words and ideas that invite readers to join in and invent their own movements in accord with and in contradiction to the author's.

Multiple voices and their apparently contradictory aims and sources may seem to stand together uneasily and to create dissonance. Philosopher Sandra Harding writes that "women *subjects and generators* of thought . . . exploit the friction, the gap, the dissonance between multiple identities."[7] Unlike Harding, I hear harmony and resonant integrity in multiple voices, and I understand simultaneity rather than gap, and flow rather than friction. *Erotic Faculties*'s pictures perform by resonating as yet another voice or narrative, to further eroticize an erotic text.

Within herself the erotic scholar does not try to distinguish the poet from the academic or the daughter from the fucker.

Themes, phrases, and images recur throughout *Erotic Faculties,* as does a drive to approach the edge of sentimentality without falling into a maudlin abyss. Popular culture loves the sentimental, which permeates game, talk, and news shows, Hollywood film, self-help books, checkout counter reading, and hit song charts. Academic culture detests the sentimental, which it deems lacking in rigor and substance, full of romantic flaccidity, the sign of emasculated intelligence or of no intelligence at all, in other words, femininity. Underlying the intellectual dismissal of the sentimental is paternalistic authorities' disgust with woman's sloppiness, and underlying disgust is fear. Although the sentimental is manifested in genres that are masculine—detective novels, rock video, adventure and sports-hero movies—as well as feminine—romance fiction, self-proclaimed New Age seers' go-with-the-flow "slop," gossip columns, and "beauty" advice—femininity prevails in (mis)understandings of the sentimental. The masculine sentimental is (mawkishly) hard-hitting, the popular equivalent of academic rigor, whereas the feminine sentimental yields so much to feeling that it falls apart, into tears.

Fear of tears is fear of erotic connection, the lush and luscious prosaic events, breath, smells, and words that people share. The academy, institutionalized into a body of Dry Eyes, is afraid of ambush by the erotic.

I am the bush, burning so hot that my words redden your ears and eyes. Red eyes are crying, they respond unwittingly, without owner consent, to the interference of emotion, a surprise attack of sentience.

Sentimental strike force, as in love as Mary Magdalene
Maudlin: tearfully sentimental; after Maudlin, Magdalene
(Middle English), often represented with eyes red from weeping
Sentimental, stroking
The strike force slops around outside the bounds of rhetorical protocol
Accused
Of trashiness exaggeration triviality
Of being chatty easy superficial anti-intellectual narcissistic
Intimate and self-indulgent
They call the strike force
Exhibitionists who show off too much heart
Too little head, the Dry Eyes say, is mush and gushy

Moist and gushy, lubricated through and through each cell and sound, the strike force asks, within the vast scheme of eros, which will outlast the rhetoric of cloistered minds, What is the difference between dreck and beauty?

I grew in my father's garden. There I learned the flowery language of lilacs, roses, pansies, honeysuckles, and bleeding hearts. I gathered the red of flowers and my mother's lipsticked mouth, of hearts both whole and broken, of blood between the legs and in the pulse, the wiseblood and the lifeblood that constitute love. Sometimes the bleeding hearts in my father's garden kept me company. Their stalks curved over shaded soil, under oaks and maples. This dark spot was the place I most liked to sit, nurturing my sorrows as if I had been born into a lonely person's life. I wanted to eat the bleeding hearts, but I simply touched them, resisting out of respect for their delicacy. Their plumpness provoked me to pinch them, but I exercised restraint, caressing each bloom with the whisper, "My beloved bleeding heart."

The dry-eyed scholar sentences herself to callousness. Fashion, formulas for academic success, and dread of being called a moralizer proscribe the sentimental, which women and men can recuperate as a feminine value evolving from erotic authority.[8] As more and more feminists have become academics, they have not intruded radically into male discursive and rhetorical convention. A few notable exceptions are Hélène Cixous, bell hooks, Mary Daly, Arlene Raven, and Trinh T. Minh-ha, but, writing and teaching under the assumed identity of male scholar, most feminist scholars have insufficiently honored or invented differences in methods and expressions for communicating knowledge. The sentimental is an important direction in this regard.

A colleague said about "Rhetoric as Canon," a chapter in this book, "You certainly have the moral high ground." His comment so surprised me that all I could say was, "It never dawned on me that morality was the issue." A person who assumed the moral high ground could only be supercilious, so her sentimentality would be suspect.

A friend in divinity school saw me perform "Pythia," also included here, and said, "That's one of the best sermons I've ever heard." His response thrilled me, because moral activity is erotic.

Sentiment, sentience, sense, and sentence share the Latin root *sentire,* to feel, perceive, sense. To entirely distinguish intellect from the senses is a mistake. Through intellect a person discriminates and evaluates, but she does so through sense and the senses as well. Sense and the senses are erotic faculties that aid intellection, spawn sentiment(ality), and inspire sentences that seduce the soul-and-mind-inseparable-from-the-body.

Images of hearts and flowers, ancient symbols of love in its emotional, spiritual, and sexual aspects, repeat in *Erotic Faculties*. Flowers' sensual and aesthetic beauty, their visual intensity, anchors the mind to ideas that they represent within a particular chapter. So does "golden voice," which appears in discussions of fluency as the ability to speak in the richness of one's own voices. "Holocaust of hearts," "(amazing) grace," "(fear of) flesh that moves," and "soul-inseparable-from-the-body" serve the same anchoring function, and in erotic scholarship catastrophe demands relief of misery, grace joins the physical and the spiritual, and the embrace of flesh that moves lessens erotophobia and misogynistic love, which is really desire for women to be static images of beauty, phallicized wonders who endure a slow death of lifelong femicide in order to deny the terrifying voluptuousness of gravity and time.

Erotic Faculties emphasizes art, sex, and pleasure, especially as they grow out of and affect women's lives. As these subjects intertwine, they create a densely layered picture of ways in which beauty, aging, women's bodies, and sexual practice and experience can influence making, interpreting, analyzing, and theorizing about contemporary art.

The little girl in the high modern house, sitting at the wooden table sized for her and her sister, very slowly turns the pages in *How to Draw the Nude*. A nearby shelf holds *How to Draw Portraits, How to Draw Animals, How to Draw Trees,* but she doesn't spend this kind of time with them. She asks her parents to take down certain books, over and over, from the livingroom shelves, such as a well-illustrated study of Picasso's art and a thin volume with an elegant reproduction of an angel she thinks is her own age. About fifteen years later she discovers that Dante Gabriel Rossetti painted the angel.

She stares for minutes at each picture in *How to Draw the Nude*, all of the female body, just as she stares not many years later, and on and off for a couple of decades, at *Playboy* nudes. She feels the nudes in her head and pelvis, in her vagina, desires them and desires herself, and she masturbates sometimes with these images in mind. In the third grade she draws Dora Maar many times. She has drawn the sensual angel too. As a graduate student she writes a dissertation titled "The Rossetti Woman." The nascent erotic scholar thinks about Rossetti's poems and paintings, but it is the latter that attracted her to her subject. She loves the Rossetti woman's large, red mouth, abundant hair, and lush beauty. The scholar's feminism does not interfere with her lust for the Rossetti women or for herself in them.

As a graduate student she becomes conscious of the implications of Picasso's virility: he was a good fucker, and he had imbued his images with brazen sexuality, as only a man can. *Her* brazen sexuality, alive from before she drew Dora Maar and always strong, could be misread so as to identify her only as a romantic or a good fuck.

She was a good fucker.

The pornerotic body subverts simple romanticism and sexualization, for it smells, smiles, bleeds, and shits, thus living beyond the boundaries of fine art's myths and murders. The pornerotic body plays with the tradition of fetishizing and sentimentalizing the female nude, but creates its own myths through autoeroticism.

In Part One, "Fucking Around," I meddle with the art world's recent veneration of fashionable theory. As the title of the chapter on "Fuck Theory" suggests, I treat theory with playful and erotic disrespect in hopes of asserting an expansive and accessible erotic theory. "Mouth Piece" offers the intimacy and passion of a sexual relationship as a foundation for theorizing female pleasure, and "There Is a Myth" critiques the fucked-up worship of artists and of men's promiscuous sexual prowess, belief in beautiful women's happiness, and confinement of eros to the private domain.

I am sure that my first memory, which I describe at the beginning of this introduction, indicates the regularity of similar experiences in my early life, a condition of warmth that my parents have provided consistently. I consider myself fortunate in this, and such good fortune gives "Fucking Around" and *Erotic Faculties* in general an optimistic voice that has not suffered from naïveté. Perhaps because of the vivid eroticism that took root in me as an infant, I have always been sexually sophisticated, in wisdom if not in practice. Sex, as acts and thoughts, as matter and energy dynamic, fascinates me and is an intrinsic part of my thinking about pleasure, art, and women. "Fucking Around" presents sexual acts, affection, aggressiveness, and fragility as well as the anguish, delights, and sensations based in knowledge of one's own and other bodies, as ways of grounding a human being's understanding of the world.

"Fucking Around" is not about a search for Great Sex or "the fuck of the century," both of which are figments of the imagination that rob the erotic of possibilities by limiting its focus. Madonna's statement, "I love my pussy, it is the complete summation of my life," is equally ludicrous.[9] Although women do need to develop genital pride, that is only part of imagining and making real erotic identities that have fucked around with prevailing modes of misogyny: people still think of cunts as stinking, and twenty-year-old women students tell me, unsolicited, that men their age call women who practice casual sex sluts. To fuck around is to discover the promiscuous nature of human identity, whose parts—body and spirit, profession and marital status, age and race, weight and health—people have unconsciously learned to aggressively distinguish from one another, to the detriment of erotic imagination.

Erotic Faculties's speaking subject could be called heterosexual, especially in "Fuck Theory" and "Mouth Piece." In today's too often oversimplified gender and feminist politics, the response to a woman's desire to be attractive to men and to enjoy sleeping with them can be negative. After I presented a piece not included in *Erotic Faculties,* a friend who had been in the audience wrote me:

> I understand or think I understand from your performance that you like fucking. But I'm not sure how to receive that information. It doesn't excite me. . . . Much of my response has to do with being a lesbian in a het-dominated culture and being without much representation in the media. . . . The content of your piece was just too het for me and I'm not sure that that is your responsibility. I just wondered what I was doing there listening to more fuck stories ("more" being that I'm constantly surrounded by the het media). You know, Joanna, all this men and women stuff—it just isn't my area.
>
> I do appreciate the image of you being the aggressive one—the seducer, the controller, the woman in control of her own sexual destiny. I think that is an important idea about your strength and a woman's strength and it is a radical message.[10]

My friend's words are a severe critique that is both legitimate and limited, and they indicate that sexual identification does not have to shut down either understanding or the erotic faculties. Not all heterosexuals submit to some absolute phallocentrism. Kissing a lover's penis is not necessarily any more phallus-worshipping than kissing his back, foot, hair, or nipple. Granted, the penis, like the vulva, is fetishized, but the penis is not the phallus, which is the fathers' law. The fathers' law does not want women to be sexually aggressive or satisfied on their own behalf. A woman's actual or assumed sexual identification does not designate whether or not she is a lusting subject or a carnal agent. If feminists and women do not seek those erotic identities beneath the names lesbian, heterosexual, and bisexual, which are at once overdetermined and narrow, then feminists and women will colonize themselves.

In an era of sexual epidemic, speaking about sexual pleasure and agency does not have the same liberatory meaning or impetus it did in the late 1960s during the sexual revolution. Today, when multiple partners and casual sex may mean death, they cannot as easily be weapons in a struggle against a repressive society. The idea of an unambiguously oppositional us—the sexual adventurers—and them—the moral regulators—is itself outdated, for, due to feminism, gay liberation, lesbian artists and theorists, women for and against pornography, Foucault, media representation of AIDS, battles over reproductive rights, and other events, individuals, and trends, we see that sexual pleasure exists within a linkage of cultural systems that house and deploy power to manage, indulge, denounce, demean, increase, and circulate sexual pleasure and the representation of sexuality. Nevertheless, the importance for a woman of speaking as a lusting subject and a carnal agent has not diminished, for women have yet to profoundly develop their erotic faculties for themselves through talking about and operating within the discipline of sex.

I am a sexist
I will fight for my sex
I will fight for your sex
For soul-inseparable-from-the-body pleasures
For my history with women and with men

Part Two, "Sustaining Body/Mind/Soul," concentrates on the rockbottom necessity that women know and love their bodies, that they innovate and develop body wisdom as a kind of erotology and sensitize themselves to the erotic as sustenance for human being, as a form of social security. "Sustaining Body/Mind/Soul" also directs attention to relationships and hostilities between women, cultural hatred of the female body, beauty as women's goal and trauma, and the use of female aging in the struggle against social femicide and for transformative practices of femininity and meanings of woman.

People, in public and private, act as if they have an obligation to speak about, indeed critique, other people's bodies. Co-workers, friends, teachers, actors, the president: no one is immune to the infectious excitement of scrutinizing someone else's fitness and to being the unknown subject of such scrutiny, which encompasses not only muscle tone and (narrow ideas of) beauty but also value as a human being. I could not help but laugh and shake my head when I noticed on 17 June 1994 that President Clinton's "pale legs" revealed by "skimpy jogging shorts" were news yet another time.[11] Pale legs frighten us, and so do ones that are too tan—melanoma—and black—terror of racial difference. We fear variety—of skin color, weight, shape—and we fear skin itself as it shows the condition of long life. We fear flesh that moves, and we have a weak grasp on beauty. Bodies that are not young, strong, and unmarked by scars, veins, and other blemishes—the signs of living and dying—are trashed. Flesh is dirty. As dirty as the earth itself, for flesh belongs to nature as much as to purifying posthuman technologies, but Americans suffer from dirt trauma. The body not only creates shit, it is shit, and when the body disproves the absolute and unerotically imagined contours and finish of a classical sculpture, it loses the grace that fantasy bestows.

A mother and her daughter and son sat in the row behind me on an airplane. He was restless and pissy, and he started looking into the ashtrays, which I notice are generally empty now that airlines prohibit smoking on planes. The mother told the boy not to stick his fingers into the ashtrays, but he obviously kept on, because she let loose with a tirade of dirt trauma: "You don't know what could be in there! It could be a heroin addict's needle, and maybe that addict had AIDS, and you'll get it, too! You would die. And you might stick that needle into your sister. Do you want her to get sick?" The woman went on with permutations of these ideas for minutes. The extent of body-fear astounded me and struck deep. For several moments the entire airplane became a repository of filth that could damage me, and I was stuck in that metal body for at least another half-hour. If the airplane was the embodiment of dirt, then so must be all the world below, where many more people lived to shoot up, fuck, excrete, sneeze, touch their forks to food on restaurant plates and leave it there, and drop into open trash cans and office wastebaskets Kleenex that had caught phlegm from their coughing. The world was a panorama of bodily horror. The body was an oceanic pit.

• • •

"Sustaining Body/Mind/Soul" counters dirt trauma, which operates at full magnitude in regard to aging and illness. In "Polymorphous Perversities: Female Pleasures and the Postmenopausal Artist," the old(er) body is shown as erotic, and in "Hannah Wilke: The Assertion of Erotic Will," in which I discuss Hannah Wilke's last art works, I consider the diseased body as an erotic body.

Erotic bodies do not exist in isolation from mind and soul. No body does, and all bodies are erotic when groomed by the sustenance of love. "Has the Body Lost Its Mind?" and "Duel/Duet," which was written with Christine Tamblyn, affirm, in the face of less optimistic and experiential theorizing than mine, that love is a tool for revolution and bears particular significance for women. Erotic scholarship makes love with words and ideas and makes love primary. In male-dominated Western culture women loathe themselves, even in a period of intense feminist activity, for they believe that they are physically flawed and sloppy. In a reshaped erotic economy women's love for themselves would not be the narcissism that isolates them from one another in jealousy and competitiveness. Rather, women would take erotic pleasure in flesh that moves, in fluids their bodies normally excrete, and in polymorphous expressions of beauty.

> I am forty-two but I am not middleaged, a word that connotes a fall from grace, from beauty in its many permutations, and I have, here in the flat and humid North, felt embarrassed by my own body and desires, but I have not gotten fat.
>
> I've worn silly slippers, so that the curve of my naked sole could not be kissed, and I have lain in bed all night with a comforter pulled up to my nose, no firm breasts or biceps available to my lover's eyes.
>
> I used to wear tights and tank tops, little skirts over bare legs, feet decorated in anklets and brightly colored high heels.
>
> The dead are covered up, buried.
>
> I think about fruit sweetening and shrinking as it ripens. I think beyond middle age to sweet old ladies, little old ladies. The fall from grace nears completion in the image of a small and cloying female, a shriveling fruit on the way to the garbage.
>
> Our language creates allegiance to the holocaust of hearts.
>
> Back in the desert, I am as naked and as beautiful as ever.
>
> I love this Queen of Eros, my mud-red menopausal blood.[12]

• • •

Loveless stories proliferate in the toxic mix of narratives that construct contemporary life.

Local newscasters exhibit five-second concern over the latest child abused and killed.

Women students tell me about paternal incest.

Co-workers belittle colleagues' work and deride the appearance of a woman professor who, in their eyes, is not sufficiently pretty to make them feel like men.

In supermarket parking lots men profess the urgency and perfection of their sexual skills to women they have never seen before.

We are pathetic lovers, filled with horror stories, which form a large part of today's mythic superstructure. The author *manqué* is everywhere, full of erotic energy channeled into perverse sexuality, into ways to fear each other and to be feared.

Most men we've known, a friend half my age and I agreed, do not know how to use their tongues and lips. She and I have more faith in women's oral talents and imagination.

Today's perverse placements of sexual energy are inappropriate, for they are aggressive minimizations of erotic faculties. The horror story is a wonderful genre, because it purges the imagination of banality. But when horror is a staple, sustenance becomes subsistence, and daily life is a form of aversion therapy: the culture will cure you of paranoia, insecurity, and free-floating fear by barraging you with terror.

The author loves stories that romance away the loveless narratives of popular culture and academic discourse. She believes in the alteration of narrative on behalf of love, in people's invention of loving stories, which requires leaping into a narrative and making it yours, locating yourself in the world by authoring yourself into it, purging the soul-inseparable-from-the-body of horror as obsession.

Erotic faculties require the activation of oracular voice, which is developed in Part Three, "Loving Stories."[13] Oracular voice can transform the status quo, which, in Part Three, is the hostile territory of narrative methods and devices that have frustrated and angered me because of their lack of love for flowery language.

Listen to my story, said the Bouquet Scholar. Let us share each other's tongues. Take my story to heart, like a short and necessary kiss. Let it untie your (k)-n-o-t-s, unwind you from the rules that make your flesh afraid to move. I may be the excited ambiguity of flesh that moves, so unlike a body, numbed by doctrinaire language, that tells the truth of boredom.

Flowery language has so many petals that scholars have been unable to count them all. Flowery language—generative language—is the language of love, a new logos, which is reason—the ability to think—unbound from rigor, which is not exactness but rigidity.

Oracular voice embodies thought as well as feeling, and it enters and lives in other people's bodies, so it is an intimate tool or weapon. The lover's and the prophet's language is oracular voice, a kind of subjunctive that tells what might be and what would happen if. That some people in the present use oracular voice means that what they say in it does not exist only in a utopian future. The struggles, caring, and vision communicated in oracular voice exist in the speaker's present because they exist in her body and mind.

Oracular voice tells what is and what can be done about it.

I am information micromatrix, communications center for the voices of electronic, immune, and ecological systems. To go by different names, to speak in different voices is to be a shapeshifter is to function as a slippage of meaning. The actuality of such fluidity proves that "Love conquers all" is a serious statement. Hate, some say, is love malformed, a skewed disposition of energy and matter that is the opposite of love. The notion that hate is love's antithesis invites easily defined enemies: you're an Arab and I'm a Jew, you're young and I'm old, you're gay and I'm straight. Hate is not love's opposite, but rather a variant, information networks stressed to distress. "Love conquers all" means that love is the implicit order of life, the absolute center of existence.

"Love" and "prophecy" are unacceptable academic and art world vocabulary. Not long ago an artist said to me, "Anything that has too much flesh and love the culture will reject." She said that I could say her work is about love, but I should not say that the love came from her. "My work comes from rage," she said.[14] Intellectuals and artists reject love and prophecy because they depart from the rationalistic thinking that is the cultural establishment's acceptable, respected, and appropriate mode of communication and that is a basis of art historiography. To a large degree, art comes from and communicates in nonrationalistic ways, but the mechanisms of art historiography, which function, too, in art criticism, inform artists' self-presentation: they know that certain vocabulary and explanations are approved.

My face grows flowers of pink and red. My mouth vomits flowers and sucks them in. I am the fucking fuschia arousing rose at the center of your heart. There no mind misconstrues pink as a maudlin color or mistakes rosiness for foolish optimism. A rose is not embarrassed by its color or its beauty.

The rose is rowdy. Flowering voices know Fuck Theory, the pink that was the rose of China Sharon Jericho. This pink is love. In the pink first meant in love, the highest state of health.

Oracular voice does not dwell in apocalypse. While its user may need to speak of catastrophe or cleansing, she focuses on humane ways out of present miseries. Love generates community, our society's common life. While electronic media function as one aspect of common life—a "virtual" community—so do actual speaking, working, and playing among people. Oracular voice is the connection a person as a citizen-lover realizes with other people. Like the original singers of Gregorian chants, the person operating in oracular voice does not perform to an audience but rather delivers on their behalf. Oracular voice, like love, means commitment.

Face me, said the Bouquet Scholar to her listener. When he did, she kissed his mouth; lips turned into rosebuds. The two then spoke in unison. *Let my words be the bloom of revolution. Not the round and round of circles that go nowhere, that repeat the same old stories under the veil of overthrow. Let this be the revolution whose axis is the heart.*

In "Loving Stories" I embrace the "enemy" of academic rhetoric by articulating its problems, warming up to them by saying, My voice moves at the speed of light, the speed of hearts falling in love. My lips move over my lips. They are moving over your lips, too, making revolution. They say (all our lips together in oracular voice), *No word spoken is ever lost. It remains and it vibrates.* Love is the answer; revolution is an erotic choice.

All or part of each chapter in *Erotic Faculties* I have presented as a performance. The audiences were members of the academic and art worlds, and I specify the location at the beginning of the notes for each chapter. Voice and costume are vehicles for connection. Attentiveness to enunciation, resonance, volume, speed, and silence create a conversational and sometimes hypnotic effect. My voice is strong and soothing, and distinct articulation maximizes the rhythm and melody of words. I am in love with sounds and their movement, and I concentrate on the overall utterance of a piece, which I hear as a complex song.

> The force that most fully expressed the conjunction of Frueh's intellect and physicality was her voice. Deep, strong, and melodious, this instrument ultimately entranced her audience. At one moment, its hypnotic richness whispered, even moaned, the secrets shared by lovers; at other times, it passionately decreed that if the critic is courageous enough, criticism and poetics can be the same thing.
>
> Marla Schor, "Joanna Frueh: 'Jeez Louise,'" *High Performance* (Spring 1989): 73

As I note in relevant chapters, in performance I occasionally sing sections of popular and folk songs to which I've changed some of the original or traditional words. Singing and whispering, which I also do infrequently, are startling, but neither they nor other vocal elements are histrionic. My desire as an erotic scholar is to let words enter an audience without intrusive theatricality, for the voice is an erotic tool that enters bodies and works in them organically.

Her articulation of each word seemed supernaturally clear to the speaker as she turned over a page of text with a movement so graceful that the paper fell from her fingers like a satin scarf. Then she imagined her voice flowing from her mouth like a river or shining like a shaft of light that could project to other planets. She wanted to touch every inch of her skin, but she could not, for she was reeling. Part of her existed only with the words she spoke, and they were carrying her away with them.

Without being overtly sexy the voice can be profoundly charming, and the more a speaker can modulate that seductiveness, the more her words and ideas will affect an audience. This is true whether the style of speaking recalls oratory in front of a large audience, intimate conversation with a friend, lecturing to a class, or sex talk with a lover.

The performances are visually minimalist so as not to obtrude, because the words are paramount. I generally stand at a podium, as for a standard academic lecture.

Costume is important because it makes clear the unity of intellect and body and it reveals the body's simultaneous strength and vulnerability.

> Although small in stature, her years of bodybuilding are evident in the sensuous lines of her body. Her black, pink, and white costume

> echoed the colors of Bourgeois's marble and connected the power and vulnerability of both women.
>
> Marla Schor, "Joanna Frueh: 'Jeez Louise,'"
> *High Performance* (Spring 1989): 72–73

My dress reveals upper body development and the speaker's flesh. An academic's costume, like many professionals' costumes, is a protective covering that armors a lecturer in the authority and power appropriate to her profession. I costume myself in different powers, which arouse the erotic faculties. As I said near the beginning of this introduction, erotic faculties enable amatory thought. My intention is not to attract an audience sexually but to charge an atmosphere erotically so that it, like a voice, can enter people.

The clothing is obviously wrong for a standard scholarly lecture. I've worn a white-leather, strapless minidress and red high heels ("Mouth Piece"), a red leopard-print unitard ("Duel/Duet"), and a black spandex minidress with a print of large roses predominantly white and magenta ("Fuck Theory"). Some or all of the clothing is form-fitting, and the colors black, red, pink, and white repeat, generally in solids. The colors frequently relate directly to images in the texts. A long poem in "Mouth Piece" is structured, in part, by the colors white, red, and black. (My hair is almost black.)

> Frueh, dressed in this delicately detailed tux, appeared like a vision [out] of Romaine Brooks's portraiture.
>
> Elise La Rose, "Vampiric Strategies,"
> *Dialogue* (September/October 1990): 25

> Frueh was her own best ad with her generous yet sleek weight-lifter's body.
>
> Nancy Martell, "Christine Tamblyn/Joanna Frueh,"
> *P-FORM* (January/February 1990): 23

I have worn a straight skirt and a jacket with a silk or satin camisole underneath. After I'm introduced or early in the presentation I take off the jacket. This gesture, or the audience's looking at skintight lycra or white leather, casts me as a spectacle that could easily be labeled "sex object," attractive according to masculine desire. But the erotic body is a voice that conveys rhythms, ideas, and sensuousness particular to an individual and not modeled by masculine standards. My intention is to convert formulaic erotic language and symbols into a foundation for erotic expansion. So I present myself as familiar erotic terrain but quickly convert it through words, ideas, and the particularities of my bodily gestures and vocal modulations into an erotic relation that turns an object into a subject who speaks and fucks in her own voice. That is a position of autoerotic and relational power, and although the images of myself I create have a stark and alluring aesthetic impact, it diminishes quickly and normalizes so that appearance does not distract an audience and body remains as an integral element of an audience's intellection.

> An hour is a long time to listen to text being read, a long time to sit in a theater with no visual stimulation beyond the contrast of dark hair, white leather, and red lipstick. But Frueh's presence is compelling.
>
> Michele Rabkin, "Joanna Frueh," *New Art Examiner* (May 1989): 60

Stage direction and pictures in *Erotic Faculties* help to evoke that "compelling" presence, which is sensual and commanding, dynamic and embracing. They establish a flavor. The stage directions are not absolute elements of performance but, rather, indications of what has happened or what might happen, how performing a particular section of a piece has felt or how it might feel.

The speaker looks as intently at her audience as they look at her. This mutuality, this spectacle of self-consciousness is a game that lovers play, trying, whether they know it or not, to expand their erotic faculties. The lover's behavior and identity are multiple and complex. She cannot confine them to a sexual relationship, for within that constraint the erotic faculties wither. Speaker with audience, writer with reader: these are erotic relationships. The erotic scholar is a lover.

Notes

1. This paragraph and the previous one are from Joanna Frueh, "Desert City" (unpublished novel, 1988), 120, 165.
2. Michael Payne, "Criticism, Ideology and Fiction: An Interview with Terry Eagleton," in Terry Eagleton, *The Significance of Theory* (Oxford: Basil Blackwell, 1990), 88.

3. Poetry or poetic language is part of the following significant feminist thinkers' work: Audre Lorde, Gloria Anzaldúa, Arlene Raven, Judy Grahn, Mary Daly, Paula Gunn Allen, Luce Irigaray, Trinh T. Minh-ha, Hélène Cixous, and Susan Griffin.
4. Audre Lorde, "Uses of the Erotic: The Erotic as Power," in Lorde, *Sister Outsider: Essays and Speeches* (Trumansburg, New York: The Crossing Press, 1984).
5. Sandra Harding, *Whose Science? Whose Knowledge? Thinking from Women's Lives* (Ithaca: Cornell University Press, 1991), 105–38, deals with the importance of embodied knowledge for feminist epistemology.
6. See Adam Begley, "The I's Have It," *Lingua Franca* (March/April 1989): 54–59, for a light discussion about academics who have turned to personalist prose.
7. Harding, *Whose Science? Whose Knowledge?* 275.
8. Robyn Warhol, "The Narratee as Other in Harriet Jacobs's Text"(paper presented to members of the Women's Studies Program at the University of Nevada, Reno, April 1994), noted that detective novels demonstrate the masculine sentimental and that the sentimental can be recuperated as a feminine value. See also Robyn Warhol, "So as You Stand, so You Feel and Are: The Crying Body and the Nineteenth-Century Text," in Frances E. Mascia-Lees and Patricia Sharpe, eds., *Tattoo, Torture, Mutilation, and Adornment: The Denaturalization of the Body in Culture and Text* (Albany: State University of New York Press, 1992), 100–125, for an enlightening discussion about sentimentality.
9. In *Basic Instinct* the Michael Douglas hero calls the Sharon Stone seductress "the fuck of the century." Madonna's statement comes from her book *Sex*, ed. Glenn O'Brien (New York: Warner Books, 1992), unpaginated.
10. The letter writer wishes to remain anonymous.
11. "Clinton Dons More Modest Jogging Garb," *Chicago Tribune*, Section I, 17 June 1994, 2.
12. This section is adapted from Russell Dudley and Joanna Frueh, "Amazing Grace," performance, 1989. "Amazing Grace" appeared in *Caprice* (July 1990): 57–72.
13. "Oracular Voice" is the title of a paper I delivered at the International Student Festival, Montage '93, Brockport, New York, July 1993.
14. Telephone conversation with an artist who wishes to remain anonymous, 26 June 1993.

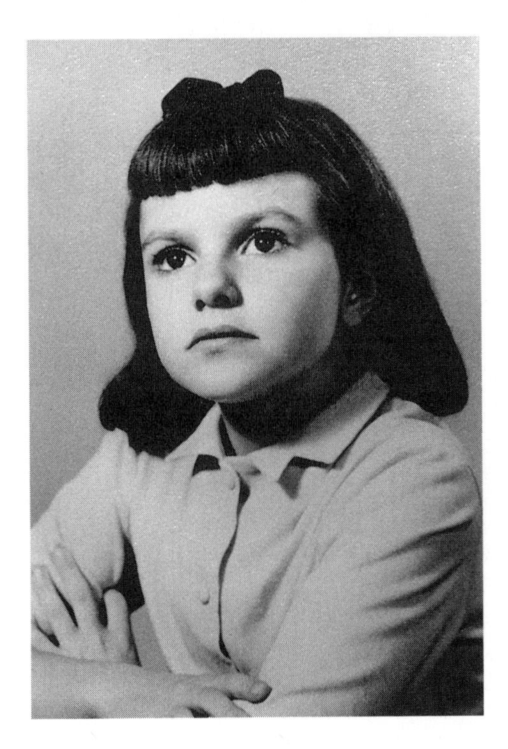

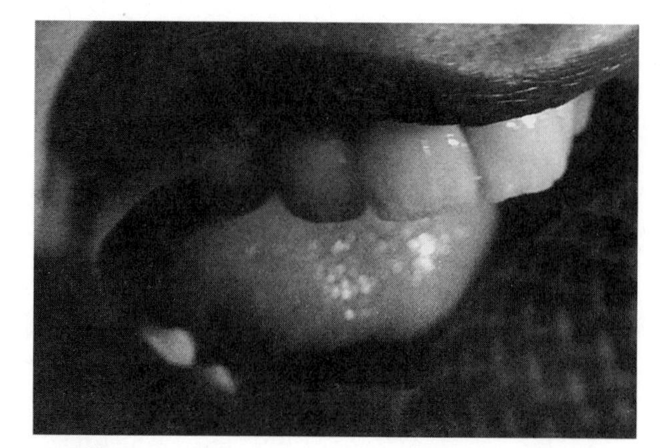

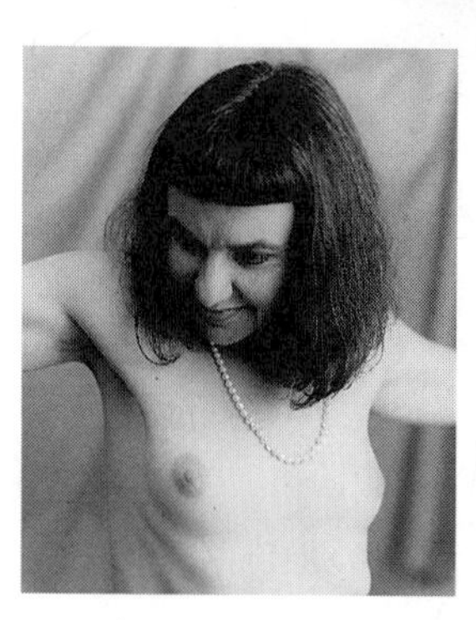

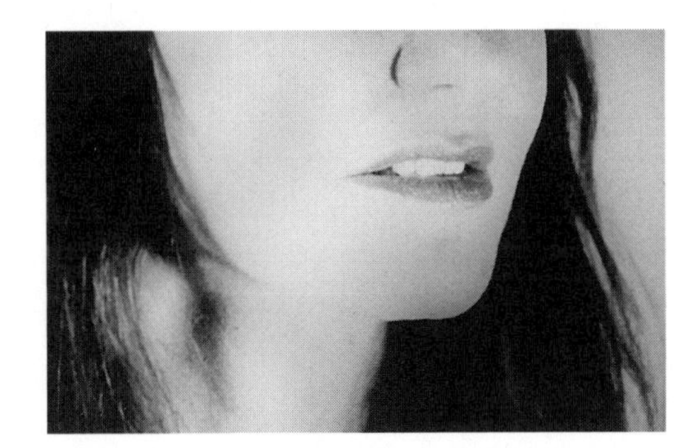

Demento Beauty, here I am
Get out of my way or I'll have to slam
Your smug little ugly little custardy face
What makes you think you're part of the human race?

CHORUS: *I'm so beautiful so berserk*
Why doesn't someone pay me so I don't have to work?
My pearlpink skin my diamondshine eyes
Miss America, move over, I'm the maniac prize

You think you're a gift to the family of man
You're a chopped up melody an also-ran
The hasbeen who climaxed before being born
If I had compassion you'd be forlorn

Demento Beauty walked the street
Ran down an alley tripped on the feet
Of a dirty condition a city of slime
Is it a corpse or a wino or just a crime?

Rape in the morning rape in the night
Look out sweet ladies or you might have to fight
The sap with integrity the guy with a gun
Who thanks you for indignities after they're done

Pull out your razorblades reach for your knives
Women of distinction buttersoft wives
Listen to the language of those hips that sway
It's Demento Beauty leading the way

I charge over bodies my arms held high
No flagwaving soldiers no apple pie
Just homemade weapons that make men twitch
The flamingo pink mouth with the tongue of a bitch

Demento Beauty, I'm so pure
Nobody's honey but I've got allure
Electro nuclear solar zap
Some say I'm magic some say a trap

CHORUS: *I'm so beautiful so berserk*
Why doesn't someone pay me so I don't have to work?
My pearlpink skin my diamondshine eyes
Miss America, move over, I'm the maniac prize

PART ONE

Fucking Around

FUCK THEORY

[*Frueh stands at the podium in a lycra minidress that bares her shoulders, arms, and chest. The dress is patterned with large roses on a black ground. Her lips are rose red.*]

The teacher liked to fuck around. She played with bodies of ideas, which she called philosophies of seduction, and with the palpitations of language. "My voice," she said to her students, "enters you as I speak, your breath and breathing fill this room, our time together. Today," she continued, "bound, wracked, and shattered hearts disturb the oblivion of Everywo/man's dreams. This is the holocaust of hearts, where the birth of fluency is daring to speak in a voice that is your own."

One of the students said to her, "You teach erotically." She took this as a great compliment but could not put her finger on the reasons for the student's statement.

The teacher, in the flesh, embodies knowledge.

. . .

The proliferation of theory has marked the art world since the early 1980s and has become one of its dominant postmodern characteristics. Many aspects of theory and its domination have irritated and disturbed me. Responsibility for a postmodern set of cans and cannots that have colored understandings of artists, art works, and art-critical writing does not necessarily lie with key figures such as Derrida, Foucault, and Baudrillard but, rather, with followers who have turned the fascinating and useful writings of father figures of speech into cant and canon. Ironically, sacred text degrades into schlock theory. Trickledown mouthings are antithetical to the relativism and eclecticism that typify postmodern thinking.

Mouthings may be sexy, but they are not erotic, for they cannot kiss a reader's or listener's soul; they are close-lipped, a fashionable attractiveness that arouses imitation. Because mouthings fail to translate ideas into the speaker's or writer's own tongue, they lack the verbal liveliness whose aesthetic configuration depends on the erotic as foundation. Fashion entrepreneur Karl Lagerfeld said, "No design, no desire."[1] This was a statement about the poor sales of American cars, but I want to give it a loving translation: style—a distinctiveness that deviates from the cant of fashionableness and that exists at one with content—manifests the erotic.

My teacher sat in front of the class smoking a cigarette and lecturing on nineteenth-century painting. Her miniskirt uncovered black fishnet stockings on crossed legs, her deep laugh spread her lipsticked mouth into a sybaritic smile, and her black hair waved witchily along paler than cream cheeks. Her dark voice slipped into my mouth and down my throat, rested on my pelvic floor and in my heart, and flashed to my extremities. With her ideas inside me, I could learn to speak perhaps as clearly as her body spoke to me.

I was in college. My teacher was Carol Duncan, a Marxist art historian with a heart on fire. She was pleasure in pedagogy.

The heart on fire is the attribute of the Renaissance Venus. Love burns in the holocaust of hearts. It can burn up or it can burn on.

I say the heart and mind are one, and the flaming heart is the intellect fired in eroticism, the intellectual who enfleshes ideas, screws around with them and makes thought voluptuous.

• • •

Baudrillard writes in "Design and Environment, Or How Political Economy Escalates into Cyberblitz" that "the great referent Nature, is dead, replaced by environment, . . . [which] designates . . . that from which one is separated; it designates the end of the proximate world." His discussion transformed my thinking about environment, but he did not lead me, in that article, to think that nature is dead. He says, "To speak of ecology is to attest to the death and total abstraction of nature" and writes, two lines later, of the "gradual destruction of nature (as vital and as ideal reference)."[2]

Several years ago I heard a photographer, in a lecture about her work, say that nature doesn't exist. In the past decade I've encountered that idea so many times in art-world wordings, often derived from Baudrillard's ideas, that I cannot cite or even remember them all. The photographer then said that only the artificial was approachable, like a golf course or a national park. I know that nature, as a word and as many ideas, is a product of the human mind; and I also know that mountains, cactuses, desert, and sunset exist. They could be seen outside the building where the photographer spoke in Tucson.

Cant demeans the reality of personal experience, which is not necessarily innocent, romantic, or devoid of intellectual astuteness.

I stood on top of a mesa and the wind said, Be my daughter or I'll blow you over the edge.

My mother saw a buck leap over the backyard fence last summer. Deer were once exotica, sights to see on family travels in Vancouver, Maine, Colorado. The strange and the familiar forever conflate, and now deer menace the garden in my parents' suburban home north of Chicago.

Last July, in my own home in Nevada, underground rumbling woke me at 4:00 A.M. Later that day I expected news reports of an earthquake or a bomb test. I asked people if they'd felt what I had. I found no confirmation.

Neither did Russell and I after he pushed me out of bed in a panic in the middle of the night when he saw a huge snake where our pillows met.

Immediate experience with spirits who embody the land is primary in some work by Southwest American Indian women writers: Lucy Tapahonso's story, "The Snake-man," updates Big Snake-man in the Navajo Beauty Way.

Nature as the great referent resonates. It figures in many contemporary stories and shifts shape according to the teller.

Nature includes the speed of light; the interactions of plants and women in the curandera, who appears as a character in Hispanic and Chicano Southwestern women's writing; the elements in plants that benefit human health and beauty; the name of a legendary stripper, Tempest Storm; the idea that, as theorist Donna Haraway says, "Our best machines are made of sunshine; they are all light and clean because they are nothing but signals, electromagnetic waves, a section of the spectrum . . . [and the] engineers [of such machines] are sun-worshippers"; the fact that the Earthquake is the name of a radio station in the San Francisco area; the techno-organism of human being and computer; my mother telling my father to cut back the dying honeysuckle on an ungardened part of their property and Dad exclaiming, "What do you mean? This is a forest!"; the Southwestern American Indian cultures understanding that sexuality and wilderness are the same.[3]

I saw a stick and it looked like a lizard. I saw a lizard and it looked like a leaf. I heard a rattler sound like a cricket. I saw a snake and it was a snake.

Things are not what they seem, for nothing is singly itself. Do not call this phenomenon the synthesis of dialectics. Call it love. Lovers know Fuck Theory.

Comet cleanser smells like cum, hawthorn blossoms smell like cunt, and evergreens, in a particular intermingling of light, humidity, and temperature, smell like human urine.

I smell. The verb is transitive and intransitive. I smell a rose. I stink.

I reek of rose. Flowery sounds enter you as I speak, my body blossoms within yours. I am Fuck Theory, the heat of the sun, the intellect alert in nerves, flesh, blood, and water, as it seduces the scent out of matter. That scent is the breath that carries a golden voice from rose and crotch and mosques whose mortar was mixed with attar of rose so that when the sun shone, the building became perfumed.

[*As Frueh speaks she hears an uncanny clarity in her voice. It is so acute and affectionate that it penetrates listeners' bones while demanding nothing.*]

In my reeking rosiness I like to wear full skirts so I can take long quick strides as though I'm walking away from the damned; and I also think that maybe I'm one of the damned and that's why I'm walking so fast.

To be good and evil is to be in between, in movement, and to be outside them altogether, to cross into them from other conditions. Crossing is the law of laws. Crossing is love, which excludes no one, nothing. Fuck Theory loves all positions.

The technical language of postmodern theory became an exclusionary weapon, a tool of mastery over art-world money-, star-, and idea-making. This situation was replete with irony, for schlock theory mouths an end to mastery. Words such as *sign, code, text, discourse, problematic, privilege, male gaze, phallic mother, hegemony, praxis, fetish commodity,* and many more have come to be part of the unloving tongue of schlock theory. Technical fields have technical languages, art being no exception, and key figures speak a magic language that transforms, on the tongues of charmed followers, into prosaic jargon that, despite its tediousness, belongs to a postmodern arcanum whose very arcaneness has been spellbinding.

Arcane language holds schlock theorists in thrall, and they make mental masturbation into the Postmodern Mysteries. Erotic thinking is also mental masturbation, the voluptuary's enjoyment of her own insatiable intellect. Erotic thinking, unlike Postmodern Mysteries, desires connection beyond the arcane legitimacy of a limited self-love. The erotic thinker is a fucker.

Years after her student said, "You teach erotically," the teacher could finally say to herself, "Now I can put my finger on the reasons for the compliment. I finger ideas the way I finger my own clit and lovers' hair. I fuck myself in public when I speak, I put my fingers on listeners' parted lips to learn better, each time I touch an organ other than my own, the fingerings of flesh that produce the clearest and most subtle fluencies. With my hand on my heart, I offer no finishing touches."

The teacher remembered a long-gone sex partner who had said to her, after she performed fellatio for a few minutes then hesitated for fear of having cum in her mouth, "Get your mouth off my dick and look at me. I'll do myself." She had cringed under his narcissistic hostility, which killed her loving tongue for him forever.

Other memories came:

The Mormon, a teacher too, who said, "Teaching is being, not information."

The psychic who said, "'Love conquers all' is no laughing matter. You give your students unconditional love."

I use the word *love* to designate certain phenomena, the fluent and stuttering connections of invisible relations among people, TVs, waters, angels, animals, antibodies, radios, deities, plants, and bodhisattvas. Love is the ultimate phenomenon, the spinal cord and spiral dance of magic, physics, spirituality, mathematics, and psychology. Love is the heart of the seemingly dismembered body of reality, for love incorporates all positions.

Love is the common ground. There nothing is a law unto itself. There human flesh is indiscrete, not boundary, barrier, or object. There a listener hears the words *threshold, indeterminacy, fluctuation, multiplicity, contingency, and in-betweenness, liminal, fluidity, permeability,* and *vulnerable* as sounds whose movement holds together sky, earth, and water in their particular configuration; joins people in sex, romance, and familial and national ties; enfolds the conscious and unconscious functions of the mind; links human and computer minds in cyberspace; keeps your blood from spilling out of your pores; creates inescapable fields of gravity light-years away; and rotates the earth on its axis.

Love makes the world go round.

I learn to dribble honey
(A moment is not absolute)
Gold starts sticking to my lips
(A century is a moment in history)

As I search for golden tongues, I meet the '49ers' gold fever, the conquistadors' greed, and Jason stealing the golden fleece. I see yellowing pages that say, "Obey the Golden Rule: do unto others as you would have others do unto you."

Our kiss lasts only a moment
Fluency is one golden moment

The unloving tongue of Postmodern Mysteries diminishes thinking that does not fit the self-made masters' constructions of reality. David Joselit's critique of Carolee Schneemann's slide installation, *Cycladic Imprints*, in San Francisco MOMA's 1991 *The Projected Image* exemplifies such distortions.

> In light of recent feminist theory, which understands femininity as a constantly shifting and transformable set of characteristics, *Cycladic Imprints* appears somewhat naive. In its dependence on supposedly timeless symbols of the female body—the violin, fertility figures, the vagina itself—Schneemann's work seems to assert that femininity is something timeless and unchanging and based on the body alone.[4]

For Joselit, Schneemann's work does not meet the social-construction-of-the-body criterion of complexity and sophistication wrought by fashionable theory. When someone does not use or refer to that obedience-demanding cant, she "appears somewhat naive." Naïveté, however, may reside in the dissolution of carnal knowing—wisdom that develops through enfleshed ideas—into displacements of the body by postmodern mouthings.[5]

Recently I talked with Carol Duncan, and much of our conversation centered on postmodern theory. She called it a radical orthodoxy. I think of postmodern cant as an amazing gracelessness.

I listen for golden voices and amazing grace. I stammer, tell only parts of stories, as any storyteller does. I am listening for self-love that cancels cant, which is the thriving sickness of self-erasure.

I look more like a whore as I grow older, act the age of ancient Graces, the sacred charismatics who gave charity as sex, compassion, kindness, all the faiths and hopes that countered culture at its worst and brought to life pornography as dirty as the earth itself.

Dying dictionaries say too simply that pornography is writing about whores. New scholars speak new meanings. They say, Pornographic partners know Fuck Theory, the powers of true love.

[*Frueh returns to the panelists' table and takes her place among them.*]

Notes

"Fuck Theory" is a revision of a performance with the same title that was delivered on the panel "Postmodernism in the Classroom: What Are We Talking About?" Society for Photographic Education Conference, Washington, D.C., March 1992.

1. Karl Lagerfeld, quoted in Maureen Orth, "Kaiser Karl—Behind the Mask," *Vanity Fair* (February 1992): 158.
2. Jean Baudrillard, "Design and Environment, Or How Political Economy Escalates into Cyberblitz," in his *For a Critique of the Political Economy of the Sign*, trans. Charles Levin (St. Louis: Telos Press, 1981), 201–2.
3. Donna J. Haraway, "A Cyborg Manifesto: Science, Technology, and Socialist-Feminism in the Late Twentieth Century," in Haraway, *Simians, Cyborgs, and Women: The Reinvention of Nature* (New York: Routledge, 1991), 153; and see Patricia Smith with Paula Gunn Allen, "Earthly Relations, Carnal Knowledge: Southwestern American Indian Women Writers and Landscape," in Vera Norwood and Janice Monk, eds., *The Desert Is No Lady: Southwestern Landscapes in Women's Writing and Art* (New Haven: Yale University Press, 1987), 174–96, for a discussion of the relationship between sexuality and wilderness.
4. David Joselit, "Projected Identities," *Art in America* 79 (November 1991): 121.
5. Margaret Miles, *Carnal Knowing: Female Nakedness and Religious Meaning in the Christian West* (Boston: Beacon Press, 1989), 8–9, writes, "'Carnal knowing' refers to an activity in which the intimate interdependence and irreducible co-operation of thinking, feeling, sensing, and understanding is revealed. . . . The consanguinity of human beings depends on mutual recognition of the common bond of a sentient body, whose most vivid experiences create consciousness."

MOUTH PIECE

[A black folding chair and music and mike stands sit upstage center. The music stands hold the script. Frueh enters, wearing a white-leather, strapless minidress, bright red high heels, and scarlet lipstick. The heels click slowly on the floor. She walks downstage center and speaks unmiked, her back to the audience.]

When I was twenty-five, I began voice lessons. My teacher's name was Everett. Everhart, strong as a wild boar, your voice was rich and mellow. You had control and power, authority and beauty, seductiveness and compassion, a heart that came from the diaphragm, source of the column of breath that rises from the gut, from the vital organs, of which the mouth is one.

The mouth, your voice said to me, is the exit from the body and the entry to the world, the opening at which the inner and the outer breath are one and private and public air can mix.

Everett gave me satin dresses, red and white and black, bought at mansion sales. I was to perform in the gowns, for Everett wanted me to be a singer, a chanteuse, creating heat with torch songs.

On the night of his sixtieth birthday, Everett came to hear me at a club. He said my singing was the best gift he could receive.

Once, early on, he told me, "You have a golden voice."

Sometime later, I said, "I want to be a star."

He said, "You will be."

Not long after that, Everett became ill and lessons were canceled week after week. When he began teaching again, I did not return. Another of his students told me, "Everett's asking about you. You're like a daughter to him." Still I did not return.

Everett, Everhart, the next time I heard about you, from a student, she told me you had died. Someone, a disgruntled lover, it was said, had knifed you in your studio, where you had moved my voice to sing and speak in ways I had not known before.

[*Frueh turns and faces the audience. From now on she alternates between standing and speaking miked and sitting and speaking unmiked.*

Standing, miked.]

Mouthpiece:

One who speaks on behalf of others; one who expresses another's sentiments and opinions; one who gives public circulation to the common soul.

Mouthpiece:

Something to put in the mouth. That part of a musical instrument which is placed between the lips and is usually made of a material agreeable to the mouth.

Mouthpiece:

An instrument in which the vibration of membranes sends forth harmonies that scholars throughout the ages have been unable to reduce into components and have therefore named aesthetics and poetics. Examples include wood wind and flesh cock.

Wood wind and flesh cock speak. They announce, proclaim, both by sensation.

I speak in public.

Seas and rivers, desert prairie speak. They reverberate, emit the sounds that scholars cannot categorize.

I speak in private.

Baying hounds give tongue and firearms report.

I speak on, against, and for.

Speak: to exercise the voice; to loosen discourse; to deliver an address in an assembly; to disclose, reveal; to appeal to, touch, affect, or influence.

I speak to desires.

I am on speaking terms with you.

[*Frueh looks directly into an audience member's eyes.*]

I speak for those of you who don't yet know the words, who've lost your tongues, who have not found your voice, who are afraid to tell your stories, fearful they may be too telling.

I will be your mouth, speak out, so as to be heard distinctly.

I will speak up, testify to acts, emotions that exist in speechlessness because belief calls them unspeakable.

I just wanna testify 'bout the love you give to me, and so I have a foul mouth, trash mouth, big mouth for speaking on the streets and in the bedrooms.

With my big mouth I can eat your heart, swallow your pride, devour you if I desire.

With my big mouth I speak in blood and shit, in cum, saliva, and orgasm, in wisdom gained through books and body.

And it was written that He was excruciatingly close to coming. "And then He came," She said. "For I drew out His semen, warm and slow, and I tasted His orgasm, I took Him wholly into Me, into the body of the world."

I speak with a learned tongue, for I am the Spokeswoman, Woman-Who-Speaks.

Belief that the feminine nature could be coarsened by learning has been coupled in history with the idea that it is in woman's nature to say too much.

[*Frueh speaks the next sentence so lightly and with such delight that she smiles. She imagines that the smile is shared by the audience and that it exists within them if not on their faces. The smile indicates mutual knowledge and experience about men's sometimes absurd and infuriating behavior.*]

Loquaciousness in the female sex has been remarked upon, not surprisingly, by the most voluble of men. Woman's wagging tongue was discussed by Aristotle, Aristophanes, Juvenal, the Babylonian Talmud,

Swift, Ben Franklin, Shakespeare, and Milton. Her silence was counted a virtue by Sophocles, Plutarch, Saint Paul, and Samuel Johnson. Babblers, tattlers, gossips, chatterboxes, nags and scolds: the descriptions apply to one sex only and suggest a severe defect of character. It is said that women gush. (Ah! But men gush. Gushers.) We run on about insignificant matters. The din is infernal. What's a man to do? A popular pub in London, The Silent Woman, named for the Ben Jonson farce, has as its tavern sign a headless female torso, a final resort.[1]

"I am Wordswoman," She said, "Swordswoman, and I use wordplay as a weapon from the head and lips. I speak in leather, as an animal, in black hair. I speak in metaphor and emblem. I speak in legend and case history, as seer, goddess, scholar."

And it is said that all who feared and loved Her listened well, for otherwise they would die in sorrow, never knowing how to speak, from Greek *spharageisthai*, to crackle, from Sanskrit *sphūrjati*, it roars, it crackles.

[*Seated, unmiked.*]

You speak of omens. I don't hear men doing that. My mother always has, and my women friends. You speak of the sexy black death snake you met on the mountain trail, on your approach to a rock you later climbed. You speak of white rabbit heads brought to you by your dogs. You speak of your own terror, and your terror speaks belief in magic, and your words themselves are speaking magic, spoken magic, the making of magic speech, the capacity to make magic speak.

[*Frueh's breath, from deep in her body, is soft. She feels as if she sighs this passage.*]

Your breath spoke to me. That was before we began to breathe hard with desire. We sat on the hood of my car and you asked me if I'd sleep with you, and I smelled your breath, your fragility. I touched your hair and cheek and you wanted to kiss me and you took my fingers in your mouth and had one hand at my waist and tucked a finger between my sock and skin. It's hard to describe how I scrutinized you. It's simply that I felt your vulnerability, and in that, your desire, so strongly that I thought, How can I? How can I do this? Sleep with you? I felt absolutely drawn, yet distant in scrutiny. I felt soft, like a balmy breeze, an angel in your arms (the wind was speaking), and I had no idea what age I was.

We made love and the rocks
Spoke
We were moving through
The rocks
We moved and the rocks
Moved with us
We were moving rocks
Moving mountains

We speak in love letters. Love alters the order of our customary alphabet.

We speak in blood letters, imagine ripping each other apart when we make love, a re-creation of ancient ritual in which the male was sacrificed.

You speak: I am your lover, you can't kill me. But cut me. Make incisions in my back, suck my blood and I'll lick yours from between your legs.

You speak in the wild, about wanting to know me in the mountain winterlands, in a sleeping bag
bedded down
my cold nose to your cheek
to take me to the snows I've never seen
so you can lace me in your love
close to the earth
my dark hair in our mouths
when we kiss

You speak in the grocery store: I want a bloody wine.

You speak in the restaurant, to the waiter: Which wine is the bloodiest?

You make the red wine speak when you pour it on and into me and sip it from my cunt and lips and let it sink into my hair so that it mats and smells like flowering soil.

[*Frueh is almost breathless.*]

. . .

When you speak, in mild words, to your mother of the magic spoken from our blood and brains and bodies, she says she sees a red flag, waving darkly like her mother's visions, feared by the family, who do not understand the source or point of prophecy, in which, it seems, you share your grandma's gift.

But your mother need not worry, for in fifty years you and I will speak together, on our golden anniversary:

You are my goldsmith
Goldmine filled with sunny dispositions
Of my wealth

[*Standing, at mike. Frueh emphasizes her upright posture and speaks emphatically, as she imagines Hypatia or Cleopatra would have spoken to a crowd.*]

I speak in milky tongues
And at the whites of eyes
White water rafter
I speak in the voice of worms
And underground rivers
I speak in dirty words in smut
The black of soil and sex
I speak goldilocks brunette and silver white and
Redhead
I White Buffalo Woman
Grow flaming snakes that crown my scalp
I speak as bête noire
As the dark horse
Running like a winner right beside you
We are in the black
Together
Making profits with our love
I speak black bear blackberry
Black swan black pepper
And black henbane hellebore and hemlock
Plants of death
I speak as queen of spades the nightshade

Black lady with my black book
Full of names of lovers young and old
Flames burning still fires
In my heart
I sound the red alert
I speak black market
Violate
The public regulations
I speak in currency betrayed
By the blackout of love
(Which I foretold)
The indecisions blind to candlelight and heavy breathing
Rhythms of the bedroom
Spreading the sky's legs
I speak white lightning
Drink white ladies
Flagrant red and drunk
I speak in black tie
Ready for a party
I am lit and flushed
Dyed bloodshot through and through
Incited and redhanded
Wanton nails turned into claws
Red rover
I speak rouged for action
Queen of Hearts
The ruby in your teeth
The cherry on your tongue
The wine you swallow
I speak Red Cross
Humanitarian
Brain coral red
And bleeding heart
I speak red-footed falcon
Who sees heartbeats of angels
Flutter in white mist
I speak black powder blasting
My way into viscera

Darkrooms
Where pictures of a golden age develop
When I speak
White dove and raven robin redbreast
I am speaking
White sheep in my dreams
And black sheep
Straying from the fold
The monochromes of cant
Though I speak lily snow and milk
The whitened head of age
Speaks too in bridal dress
The white nun orchid
    showy
        breathing in the tropics
        bearing single icy flowers
        suffused with rose
    Snow White enough
The bride in Ivory Soap
She is the bitch too wearing white as well
As her unbridled passion
Red hot mama
        eating white and devil's food cake at my wedding
I speak in gold stars
Slice golden sections
For a new gold standard
For I am the black
Remains after the fires have burnt out
I am the white
The ashes blown
I am the red
Mouth at your ear and belly
        Telluric
I speak pitch darkness
Bloody tongues
White magic
See these lips?
Look at my mouth move over every word

And all I say is golden
Like the marigold and palomino
[*Frueh sings. Her eyes are closed most of the time.*]
Black black black is the color of my true love's hair
His lips are like some rose so fair
His eyes speak gold when'er we talk
I love the ground whereon he walks

[*Seated, unmiked.*]

You sing to your dogs, Ananda, Pup, Xia Wu, personalizing rock songs for their pleasure.

Ananda's got the snake
Pup's on the take
Xia Wu's on the make.

Then you choose a rap song, sing it deadpan:

Trick and magic
Magic trick
We're Mame and Joey
And we like it slick

You say you're not sure if you remember the women's names right. I say it doesn't matter, they sound great and, besides, you know my name perfectly. You whisper it when we're fucking and I'm on top of you. Over and over, Joanna Joanna Joanna Joanna, and it becomes a soft cry, like Oh God or Jesus, which are sometimes louder, but not as loud as screams.

Often when I think about everything we do with sex, I want to scream, and I wonder, Are our sex sounds and words a song?

[*Standing, at mike.*]

Sing:

From Middle Welsh *deongl*, to explain, Greek *omphē*, voice, oracle, and probably Prakrit *samghai*, to say, teach.

Sing:

[*Frueh lets the sentences sound like music, proclamation, chanting, and a voice making love.*]

To utter words in musical tones, inflections, modulations.

To proclaim in a clear or resonant manner.

To chant, intone, to celebrate.

To make love with words, make poetry.
To bring or accompany to a state by singing.

[*Frueh crosses her arms and holds herself.*]
I will sing you to eternity and back
I will sing away your pain
O Goddesses
O Gods
Eros Astarte
Songsters
Songstars
It's the singer not the song
We come
To sing your praises
Tell us of the torch songs
Intoned at first for martyrs
Final songs for lover men aflame
Like saints and witches
Bound to twigs and branches
Sticks and flesh both named faggot
faggot faggot faggot faggot
Sing forgotten songstars
Sing Choir of Angels

Etymological relations among passion, fury, song, excitement, violently desiring, raving, burning with love, storm, to understand, possession, god-inspired singer, oracle, being-outside-oneself, and poetry characterize the creative aspect of the unconscious, whose activity sets human beings in motion, overpowers them, and makes them its instrument. Human beings are seized by these powers. But since this possession causes higher, supraconscious powers to appear in human beings, they methodically seek it in ritual, in art, religion, cult, in sex and poetry.[2]

The semiotic chora is the site of those meanings and modes of signification that cannot be reduced to the symbolic order and that exceed rational conscious subjectivity. The semiotic chora is manifest in symbolic discourse in such aspects of language as rhythm and intonation and is at its strongest in nonrational discourses which threaten the organization of the symbolic order and the stability of its meanings, such as unorganized religion, art, and poetry.[3]

Oracular priestesses, who were originally associated with sacred poetry, were each called *saga*, She Who Speaks. *Saga* literally meant female sage.

[*Seated, unmiked. Frueh crosses her legs and leans forward with one arm along the back of the chair.*]

You tell me, "Never underestimate your voice." You say the first time you saw me you were taken by my voice, the sound, the words, the short and rose-red boots whose curving to my ankle you describe with lyric lust, my mouth which you presumed I lipsticked scarlet as a sign of vocal clarity, my entire being read by you as voice.

[*Frueh leans back.*]

And I listen to the cadence and the colors of your voice, the songs you make of daily life.

And I think, We speak with each other in the voices of angels. Your body and mine are vocal organs.

[*Standing, at mike.*]

The celestial voice exists in every human being and can be expressed individually or by vox populi. Communities are vocal organs composed of people who know they have a voice. (They listen to their inner voices and to the voice of winds.)

We can pinpoint a major hindrance to the development of the celestial public voice in the psychological evidence manifested in high school students' English essays. Recent studies reaffirm older data: only the rare student consistently uses the active voice. Ideas in both logic and poetry suffer from passive sentence structure. Our conclusion is that people who do not feel they are agents in their own lives have difficulty understanding the active voice, in sentences and in society.

Unfortunately, many teachers are no exception. They have memorized the principle, but they have no voice.

[*Frueh speaks deliberately and gently.*]

Words and their content may expand the abstract, intellectual portion of consciousness, but ideas alone do not and cannot cause change. The teacher's voice vibration can augment the experience of learning, and it is the sound, which could as well be gibberish or chanting, that brings the change. The control and mastery of sound waves is part of the path of a teacher. Thus the teacher can talk about anything at all, can sing, moan, cry, or laugh and still achieve results.[4]

[*Seated, unmiked.*]

When we are miles apart, one of the things I miss most about you is your laugh, your many laughs. They are contagious. You infect me with your love.

[*Frueh is excruciatingly aware of walking across the stage.*]

[*Standing, at mike.*]

The mouth is the gateway of infection. We share food and blood and air, drink and cum and kisses.

What follows is part of the case history of a contemporary Don Juan, whom I refer to as X.

As X entered his twenties he became sexually hyperactive. At twenty-five he began to use heroin regularly, and often he shared needles. Both practices put him in danger of contracting AIDS.

A new sex partner said to him, "I'll kiss you anyway." Then she performed fellatio. She pulled back, which angered X, and he said, "If you're afraid, you don't have to finish me off. Watch me do it." When X ejaculated in his hand, the woman said, "What a narcissist." X smiled.

The Black Death scourged Europe six centuries ago, and Edgar Allan Poe has written of the Red Death. But I will tell you a story from the nightmare days of the White Death, when milky-colored pustules signaled someone's end.

One town built a wall around its borders before the plague struck. A woman named Head of My Heart begged the mayor to leave the gate open till Hope in One Eye returned from business travels. He was due that very day, and Head of My Heart and Hope in One Eye were best friends. The mayor and all his deputies would not listen to Head of My Heart, nor would they let her leave. Did she want her town to die for love of one man? Would she die for love? She could not answer, did not know if love of one was worth the death of many.

Three years passed. The gate flew open, as if it knew the plague itself had died, and Head of My Heart left to look for her friend. She did not find him anywhere, in her twelve years of searching. Mass death does not leave single graves, nor do the unwanted stay close to home.

Head of My Heart sat on the ground, the hardest she had walked since leaving the walled town, and cried. "If only love were of epidemic proportion," she said, clearly through her tears. And then she smiled, not knowing why.

[*Seated, unmiked.*]

I have two pictures of you grinning, which I took. You look like a friendly Marlboro Man. Your little teeth are very white.

When you grabbed my hair with those teeth, on the hood of my car, I could feel what a bunch of it you held. You were sitting behind me, then leaned into my back, and you pressed your teeth against my neck, maybe letting go of many strands, and bit it through my hair. I moaned and knew from then on that I held you fast, as if I had bitten into your heart before that night.

So I say, Bite me
Make me smart
With love.

And you request my bite below your nipple, as hard as I will dare.

[*Frueh uncrosses and recrosses her legs.*]

We make our marks on each other's skin. I see bruises left from my teeth in your upper arm. You bite my head, leaving a sign on my scalp that only I can see, for it is hidden under my hair.

We make our marks inside the skin. We bite each other to the core, where Eve bit into the red apple, into Adam's center too, beneath the grip of a lonely and hardbitten tyrant god.

You say when I suck your cock the second morning that we're lovers, "You're very conscious of teeth. I've never been with someone so conscious of teeth."

"Do you want more teeth?" I ask.

"No. Not now."

Then you pause and say, "Sometimes more, sometimes less."

. . .

[*Standing, at mike.*]

"Philosophers have said some crazy things about the real world. Aristotle insisted, for reasons I can only guess at, that women have fewer teeth than men. In medieval representations of him, Aristotle is often depicted on all fours, being ridden by a woman with a whip in her hand. This was Phyllis, the mistress of Aristotle's pupil, Alexander. One might suppose, from his posture of erotic domination by a woman he was mad about, that Aristotle would have believed she had more teeth than men; thus even masochists can be sexist. In any case, one need only look into the nearest female mouth to refute that mighty thinker."[5]

Armed to the teeth
Wordswoman never bites her tongue
Tooth-gnashing
She bites off what she can chew
And sits, teeth set
While tooth-winged butterflies
Circle her head like halos
[*Frueh's lips are set in a snarl.*]

[*Seated, unmiked.*]

I put my tongue against my teeth
To speak
I put my tongue to your teeth
Rub it along them
Your lips yielding
Our compliant hearts

You've worn lipstick when we fuck. The first time, you asked, after we'd been naked and in bed already for a while, "Where's your lipstick?"

I answered, "In my purse."

I turned over, on my stomach, aware of my ass in the air, to your eyes. I found my lipstick, pulled the top off, twisted the crimson stalk up, to paint your lips. Then I said, "Put it on me," and you covered my mouth with pressures like your kisses. I reddened one of your nipples and slid the lipstick over your prick, and then we kissed until I saw that the color had disappeared from your mouth.

Months before we're lovers, you see my lips imprinted on a letter. You remember them to me and say how soft and warm my lips seemed on the paper, how jealous you were of their receiver. Our second day as lovers, I kiss your chest with lipsticked mouth, not realizing anyone could see my love between the sides of your unbuttoned shirt. Unexpectedly you meet our friend Mercedes, who laughs and says, "You have big red lips on your chest." And you tell her, "Everything is different. My life has changed."

You want your own page filled with kisses. You say it will make you feel secure. I reapply the color several times for you. I lick the paper like I'm tracing veins, remembering tendons and your creamy ass and back. I drag my tongue along the dryness—only paper. My mouth forms patterns, puckered, heavy, light, and open.

Two old lovers give you grief about wearing what you call your "snazzy lipstick" in public. One asks, "Do you want to get beat up? I'd feel safer walking alone at night than with you." The other calls you a little fuck, a term I find it endearing that you call yourself.

You tell me that your lipstick threatens them, because you've taken on femininity and, in that, freedom.

[*Standing, at mike. Frueh touches the mike stand with the fingertips of both hands.*]

In a garden
Judas passed the Kiss of Death
With flowers all around called Kiss-Me
(Known by another name, Wild Pansy)
Christ speaking
        lip-love
        lip-homage
        in lip-lusciousness
        or was it simply lip-deep
    could have said
Just kiss my ass
I would have
She Who Speaks
With kiss-curl on the cheek

might have said
Had I been asked
Oh, honey, I will give you Great Lip Service
All you need forever

"A woman 'touches herself' constantly without anyone being able to forbid her to do so, for her sex is composed of two lips which embrace continually."[6]

Lip:

Probably related to Latin *labium*, *labrum*, lip, and to Latin *labi*, to slide, glide.

[*Seated, unmiked.*]

Almost as soon as your prick was sliding in me, as we were sliding along your prick the first time, you said, "I love you."

Prickslide: this is your word.

You call me Joanna the Slippery. I like this, my cunt wet for you, for our smooth talking.

Joanna the Slippery, the unclassifiable.

I put my finger in my cunt, in and out, slowly, as we're talking on the bed, then to my mouth, and taste, lick it, almost as if I'm not aware of what's happening, as if we do and don't know what I'm doing. But you groan.

I put my finger in my cunt, then to my mouth, and taste. Lips to lips.

[*Standing, at mike.*]

The positive femininity of the womb appears as a mouth; that is why "lips" are attributed to the female genitals, and on the basis of this positive symbolic equation the mouth, as "upper womb," is the birthplace of the breath and the word, the Logos.

Even today sexual symbolism is still colored by alimentary symbolism. Hunger and satiety, desire and satisfaction, thirst and its slaking are symbolic concepts that are equally valid for sex and for nourishment.

. . .

Magic began no doubt as "food magic" and developed by way of fertility magic into sexual or "love magic."

The goddesses of love, the hunt, and death are grouped together in Egypt as in Greece, in Mesopotamia as in Mexico. Symbols of the womb-as-underworld include the gate and gully, the door, ravine, abyss, and, of course, the gullet. All are numinous sites. The mouth with bristling teeth and the gullet actively rend, swallow, devour, and kill. The toothed vagina's sucking power is mythologically symbolized by its attraction for man, for life and consciousness and the individual male, who can evade it only if he is a hero, and even then not always.[7]

It is said, "When Woman Who Speaks says, 'Eat me,' those who listen receive oracles from her mouth."

Yet others say, "A man who gets sucked into female ways will pine and die, will be no true man, in fact, nothing. . . . Our myths illuminate the facets of this stereotype."[8]

Woman Who Speaks says, "The hero enters to be devoured. If he survives with true desire, he returns, at once diminished and engorged."

[*Seated, unmiked.*]

You tell me, "I was talking to you, out loud, in my bed."

"What did you say?" I ask.

"I want your cunt to devour me. I want your mouth around my dick when it's nonexistent."

[*Frueh wants to pause a long time—thirty seconds—because the previous statement amazes her.*]

I'm astonished that someone called a man would say this.

Later you send me a letter. All it says is, Gorge-us.

Part of a story I wrote scares you. You say the heroine eats up young men.

Still, you taste my menstrual blood. It is your red badge of courage.

[*Standing, at mike.*]

"Love is not blind," the Buddha says. "Indeed, only the Lover is fully aware of the Beautiful."

• • •

Wordswoman says, "The Lover sees with the mouth. The seer tastes the lover, for sight is simply another tongue, another language of the senses. The Lover sees the Beautiful, sees beautifully, has the best, the most beautiful of taste."

The appetite fails when we fall in love. The food is the lover, the lover is the food. This has to do with eating the lover, cum, sweat, tears, saliva, blood and soul-inseparable-from-the-body, the lover who is the object of appetite, desire. This has to do with wanting the smells of the lover's body. (Aroma increases appetite.) But also the lover is full of the beloved, full of love, so full that she requires no other sustenance.

Lovers eat together in public in order for everyone to see their lust, their taste, their devouring of sex.

The appetite fails because lovers have consumed each other.

[*Seated, unmiked.*]

On our first date, our first dinner out, the waiter waits, for over an hour, till we order.

You suck my fingers later
On the hood of my car
My four fingers
All but my thumb
In your mouth
It was deep wet
Saliva on each one
And you say that
You are wet
And you say that when you drink you are in my mouth.

And on the city streets we stuff food in each other's mouths and suck it out in kisses, drink liquids too this way.

And we are fucking, you on top of me. Sweat from your forehead is raining in my mouth. I lick the salt from your cheeks.

You write to me about vanilla pain. It is the taste of desire for an object out of reach.

I am eating breakfast at a cafe, where I like the coffee and the blueberry muffins. The coffee is rich, the muffin flesh melts in my mouth. I remember winter and the coffee's heat, its creamy denseness. I think of you in another climate. I am far away from you in miles. I just wrote a post-card, words I'd rather speak in your presence. I say to you, We could eat here together. We could stare at each other full of lust, and you would put your finger to my mouth, a little between my lips, wanting entry. You like to look at me in public as though you're ready to fuck me. I say to you, People look boring here. This is the dead place. My mouth is on yours when I say this. Do you feel it?

The food goes tasteless in my mouth. And I'm aware of the saliva. There seems to be more than usual, a displacement of tears?

[*Standing, at mike. Frueh speaks matter-of-factly.*]

What follows is my transcription, from a tape-recorded session, of the patient's poetic mania regarding her father.

[*Frueh fingers the edge of the music stand, on either side of her script.*]

I eat to live. But how can I live if I feel sugared to the bone? I had no Sugar Daddy who'd feed me with phrases of honor for my beauty, sex, or girl-childishness. Oh, Daddy, I sever my sex and guts from you. I sever the connections, cords, and filaments between our vital organs, the places from neck to crotch that just can't cover our insecurities. Still we speak and eat together.

I eat to live. I eat sweet to live well. I eat sweet to live at all, Oh, Sugar Daddy God My Father. I transcend the grief of stunted love by eating

cakes and cookies
ice creams
toast with butter and raspberry preserves
(your favorite fruit)
muffins, mousse, and chocolate kisses.

Where were yours? There would have been no incest in the meeting of our father-daughter tongues, our separate languages in words of love. The crime is in the lack of language

melting over hearts
the hot fudge sundaes I needed
melting my snowy heart into the
cream I share with men, my cum
my husband lover says is sweet.
He eats to live, eats me to live.

I eat to live. I gain no weight. I'm neither fat nor ugly, but I worry for my health, all that sugar coating me inside like silken death. I am too sweet, not sweet enough. Was I not sweet enough for you? Am I, I wonder over twenty years, a poison in men's veins as soon as their eyes taste me?

[*Frueh embraces herself and caresses her upper arms.*]

I eat to live. But I'm so sick of sweets, for every day cannot be Valentine's, plump hearts and flowers candied for supposed lovers.

I eat to live. I try to make myself sweet, but there's no cure for hunger like this, the rotting sweet tooth of a daughter, except to say, Dad, I love you and I must let go, cut our umbilical cords. To let go we embrace anew. In letting go we come together cleansed of all the saccharine father-daughter feelings and others falsified as ugly lust, too true to publicize, destigmatize into the necessary passion of simple nurturance and occasional feast.

I eat to live. I love you, Daddy, let me be sweet enough for you. Tell me I'm sweet enough for you, so I don't have to eat as if there's no tomorrow for us. Oh, let the love, the words be sweet enough.

[*Seated, unmiked.*]

During our first dinner, we take the words out of each other's mouths, we eat each other's words and know we're gifted in each other's tongues.

When your tongue is in my cunt, I'm amazed I don't know which are your lips and which are mine, that I can't tell my cum from your saliva.

Prickslide and cunt worship are two tongues we speak. Your prick is your tongue that finds and makes a language inside me. Your tongue becomes my tongue, our prick and our cunt, and we create a language of our own, but known in variations to all loving fuckers.

[*Frueh feels lightheaded, afraid she may sway and fall over, so she makes a point, to herself, of renewing her commanding posture.*]

[*Standing, at mike.*]

With her outspread legs, the Gorgon takes the same posture as the exhibitionistic goddesses. Her outstretched tongue is always phallic. In New Zealand the outstretched tongue is a sign of power, and in Lifu, one of the Loyalty Islands, the male sexual organ is known as "his word," an expression that gives the phallus meaning as the originating force of language.[9]

• • •

Tongueman and Woman Who Speaks chose one another as consorts. In the ancient days of their love, Tongueman meant speaker, orator, and Woman Who Speaks herself spoke far and wide and wet and deep and hard. On their wedding day, she moaned in beauty through the world that worshipped her and Tongueman,

Let the organ in your mouth
Resonate in the cathedral with no walls
[*Frueh pictures her mouth as a cave, reverberating with sound.*]
The center of me my voice my being
Nexus
Confluence of the wordstreams

[*Seated, unmiked.*]

You were talking about us, and then the river. You were talking about yourself and your work, and then the river, being like the river. And you were crying, kayaking, underwater, almost drowning. As you sobbed, I watched your cheeks turn red, and I noticed your skin begin to burn, to look as though iris petals growing underneath your skin were surfacing. The petals looked like tongues, and I remembered the name of irises in the botanical garden. Scarlet Showman. Maybe this is you.

Showman
Shaman
She-Man
I go to the gardens
In my red lipstick
The wind is blowing
And shifting direction.
I come to know the language of the irises
I begin by listening to their posture
Here they stand
Some almost to my waist
Like you kneeling,
Head up, tongue offered to me,
Like you in the shower
At my cunt with your tongue.
I call them by their names

Which also sound the meaning
Of our love
  Occult
  Sun Fire
  Gift of Dreams
  True Bliss
  Serene
  Bride's Halo
  Danger
  Sorceress
  Allegiance
  Limpid Harmony
  Star Walker
  Morning Thunder
  Gypsy Magic
  Sable Night
  Chérie
  Clearfire
  Spun Gold
  Truly Yours
  Star Queen
  Royal Magician
  Black Madonna
  Blood Dance
  Heat Pump
  This I Love
  Black Gamecock
  Beaver Lass
  Trice Blessed
  Red Echo
  Bridal Passion
  One Accord
  Sweet Deal
  Star Studded
  Coral Chalice
  Marvelous Style
  New Kinda Love
  Toujours

Exhilaration
Rosy Wings
Black Flag
Night Lady
Piping Hot
Embraceable
Infinite Grace
Crystal Cathedral
Cameo Wine
Enchanting
Whispering Breeze
Deep Fire
Rosecraft
Mulled Wine
Simple Pleasure
Precious Moments
Majestic Beauty
Divine Guidance
Venus Rising
Jeweled Starlight
Sheer Poetry

[*Seated, holding mike.*]

We sat outside with your dog, Xia Wu, between us. We were watching for shooting stars. Word said there would be many. The wind blew up as we were sitting.

I lifted Xia Wu's ear, bent close so that my lips touched velvet skin, and asked if she saw shooting stars.

You lifted her other ear and said, "Xia Wu, I see one. Over there."

And as we softly talked into her ears, the wind embraced the three of us and stars shot and showered on every side.

"The stars aren't falling," I said to Xia Wu, "they're finding new homes."

Then we heard the voice, of Everett, Everhart, encircling us, for just a moment, in the wind.

"Golden voices," Everett said, "my stars."

[*Frueh lays the mike on the music stand and walks offstage, high heels clicking slowly on the floor.*]

Notes

"Mouth Piece" has been performed at:
Columbia College Dance Center, Chicago, Illinois, February 1989
Pennsylvania State University, State College, Pennsylvania, November 1990
Massachusetts College of Art, Boston, Massachusetts, February 1992
The LAB, San Francisco, California, January 1993
Syracuse University, Syracuse, New York, February 1994

An excerpt from "Mouth Piece" was published in P-FORM *(Winter 1991) and is reprinted by permission of* P-FORM.

1. I have altered this passage from Susan Brownmiller, *Femininity* (New York: Simon and Schuster, 1984), 111, in two ways. In Brownmiller the end of the first sentence I quote reads, "It is in woman's nature to talk too much." Also, I add, "Ah! But men gush. Gushers."
2. I have altered and condensed four paragraphs from Erich Neumann, *The Great Mother: An Analysis of the Archetype*, trans. Ralph Manheim (Princeton: Princeton University Press, 1972), 297–98.
3. I have altered one paragraph from Chris Weedon, *Feminist Practice and Poststructuralist Theory* (Oxford: Basil Blackwell, 1987), 89.
4. I have transposed and paraphrased W. Joy Brugh, *Joy's Way: A Map for the Transformational Journey* (Los Angeles: J. P. Tarcher, 1979), 70.
5. Arthur C. Danto, "Approaching the End of Art," *The State of the Art* (New York: Prentice-Hall, 1987), 210.
6. Luce Irigaray, "This Sex Which Is Not One," trans. Claudia Reeder, in Elaine Marks and Isabelle de Courtivron, eds., *New French Feminisms: An Anthology* (New York: Schocken, 1981), 100.
7. The preceding paragraphs in this section are a transposition and alteration of material in Neumann, *The Great Mother*, 168, 170–72.
8. Robin Tolmach Lakoff and Raquel L. Scherr, *Face Value: The Politics of Beauty* (Boston: Routledge and Kegan Paul, 1984), 212.
9. In this paragraph I have altered Neumann, *The Great Mother*, 170.

THERE IS A MYTH

[*Frueh's tone is alternately delicate and caustic.*]

There is a myth.
It says The Story of Art is for everyone
I say Men the self-enfablers call themselves Genius Master
I say They write love letters in the pages of art history

There is a myth.
It says The work of the Masters is a revelation
I say Revelation is revolution, around and around in circles

There is a myth.
It says There is no expiration date on the glories of dead men
I say All flowers wilt

There is a myth.
It says New York is magic
I say Medicine women climb Western canyons
I say New Mexico is the Land of Enchantment

. . .

There is a myth.
It says Climb another rung
I say Stop running, the race is won

There is a myth.
It says There are no more heroes in art
I say We don't need another hero

There is a myth.
It says The cream always rises
I say I am tired of rising and falling stars

There is a myth.
It says You are better than I am
It says I am better than you are
I say We exist in equilibrium

There is a myth.
It says We are evil
We belong to the darkness and
The darkness is bad
I say We turn the lights off
And call what we see obscenity
I say Touch your fear, come clean,
And the darkness and the light will no longer oppose each other

There is a myth.
It says Balls to the walls
It says The girl's in heat got that backseat beat
It says I travel the world
I've seen a million girls
I say Cunt to the front
I say The boy's in heat got that backseat beat
I say I've been around the block
I've seen a million cocks

. . .

There is a myth.
It says Blondes have more fun
I say Marilyn Monroe killed herself
I say Jean Harlow's husband beat her
I say Jayne Mansfield was decapitated in a car accident

There is a myth.
It says Woman is Other
It says The husband is the head of the wife
It says The penis is the head of the body
It says Men are fuckers, screwing into some dead,
Dark female core, penetrating the heart of the world of ideas
It says Woman is absent, she is a cunt, a nothing, a black hole
I say I am a fucker
I say I am a cunt, and I speak with my own body
I say The phallocrats are thoughtless
I say They talk big, they talk too much about big things
I say They fear their smallness, their own absence
I say I am a woman, and I have more presence than you have absence
I say Call me the living

There is a myth.
It says Those who build their bodies are dumb
It says They who develop their minds are weak
It says You whose hearts grow deep roots will bleed
I say There is a three-in-one
A triple goddess, a trinity
I say I am a bodybuilder, thinker, bleeding heart

There is a myth.
It says You are human
I say Turn into a wolf
I say Start howling now

There is a myth.
It says Eroticism belongs in the bedroom
I say I am Eros and you are Eros and
We can kiss, tongues deep in each other's mouths, whenever we please

. . .

A friend gave me a card. It was deep violet. She had written on it in silver the following words:

The reality of the
imagined:
a complex weaving
through layers
Keep moving power full heart

I say

[*Frueh whispers.*]

LISTEN

Notes

"There Is a Myth" was given at the forum "Angry: A Speakout," College Art Association Conference, New York, New York, February 1986, and it has been delivered at the end of several performances between 1986 and 1992. An excerpt from "There Is a Myth" was published in Women Artists News *11 (June 1986) and is reprinted by permission of Midmarch Arts Press.*

PART TWO

Sustaining Body/Mind/Soul

POLYMORPHOUS PERVERSITIES

Female Pleasures and the Postmenopausal Artist

[*Wearing a form-fitting minidress that reveals her shoulders and arms, Frueh assesses the audience. Her pearl necklace and bracelet are visible to them, as are her sheer black stockings and short black boots with low heels.*]

In *The Sadeian Woman and the Ideology of Pornography* Angela Carter writes, "It is in this holy terror of love that we find, in both men and women themselves, the source of all opposition to the emancipation of women." In *D. V.*, Diana Vreeland states, "The beauty of painting, of literature, of music, of *love* . . . this is what men have given the world, not women."[1] I vehemently agree with Carter and disagree with Vreeland. The circulation of love, within the bodies of women and within civilization, which supposedly sustains human life, accounts for the (im)possibilities of pleasure. Vreeland turns love into a misogynistic joke against women, for to claim love as men's invention is to hate women and implicitly to laugh at their displays of passion and creations of pleasure in art or in life, to infantilize them, and to turn them into sphinxes—mysteries and monsters.

Reconceive the monster. She is an emancipatrix in her perversities, a muse of beauty and hilarity, a circulator of love.

Research and conversation tell me I would be unwise to generalize about postmenopausal women. But society's erotic and aesthetic aversion toward old(er) women drives me to speak for their pleasures, to theorize them, and to situate this material in my continuing development of a feminist erotics. I base my ideas on four areas of study: looking at and loving old(er) women, the experiences and art of women visual artists over fifty, feminist writings on female pleasure and eroticism, and literature on menopause and women's aging.[2] My desire is to make connections between visual pleasure and female pleasures from a position of difference, female aging, that is a largely uncharted territory, outside cultural maps of conventional femininity, and that consequently may provide feminism with new models of female pleasure.

Theorizing Observation

I remember grandma with her silver-white hair in a French twist.

She faces me in a white mink coat, wearing a diamond wedding ring, pearl necklace and bracelet. Five feet tall and unmadeup, my grandma embodies an oxymoron, unpretentious opulence.

After grandma died Aunt Sylvia and I found raspberry suede gloves in grandma's dresser. Sylvia asked, "Do you want them?" I said, "No." I was a fool.

But the diamonds and pearls have become mine, the link to a love-site of visual pleasure, my grandma, the legacy that charges me to articulate how seeing and being an old(er) woman need not be disjunctive.

Often the old do not like to recognize themselves, for aging can be a process of "adaptive repulsion" that may indicate psychic ill health.[3] Getting used to the mirror's "ugly" reflection may give in to the social incorrectness of embodying a difference, old(er) age, that is more apparent and more deeply felt by people than that between the sexes. The young(er) woman wants to be seen, the old(er) woman is hypervisible, yet, paradoxically, erased by society's alienation from its aging bodies.[4]

In my Performance Art class, women students in their early twenties talked about beauty. They cited beautiful old(er) women—a grandmother, Georgia O'Keeffe. Then one asked, with witty humanity, "But do you want to look like that?"

I catch myself staring at an over-fifty woman in a conservatively patterned miniskirt that matches her blouse. She leans on the counter in a SoHo gallery and runs her fingers through wheat-in-moonlight hair. I turn away, embarrassed to be scrutinizing a gesture and a look that seem forcedly sexy. Then I question the force of sociovisual conventions—only young(er) women can assume the appearance and postures of sexiness—and of two wishes: that her sexuality disappear and that her desire for her visual pleasure in herself not compel me to look at her.

I revise my fearful need for her and other old(er) women to age gracefully, a euphemism for fading away, lulling lust. Grace derives from Latin *gratia*, a pleasing quality. An old(er) woman who doesn't act her age is not pleasing, unlike a young(er) woman in the guise of femininity, because the old(er) woman exposes her pleasure, which society tries to deny and names indecent.

Gratia also means thanks.

Amazing grace.

I thank the woman in the gallery for the indecency of defiance.

I watch my cosmetologist's hands as she prepares to give me a facial. She grooms them as glamorously as she does her face. Deft knowledge about beauty rituals need not hide age, nor does it necessarily betray submission to the cosmetic industry. My cosmetologist's hands declare attentiveness to detail: the contrast between lightly tanned skin, mottled by darker spots, and madder red polish, the just-this-side-of-exotic nail length, the well-lotioned skin. I respond to the thick veins underneath as one more element in a picture of lush softness and lucid style.

Love of color and texture is not a crime that old(er) women commit against themselves. Old(er) women's self-aestheticization is autoerotic action and event that destroy visual pleasure as we have known it.[5] For the postmenopausal woman cannot be the feminine fetish, eroticized by patriarchal womb-worship. The nonreproductive woman's self-aestheticization deaestheticizes Woman as socially constructed femininity.

In society's eyes the old(er) woman who costumes herself in feminine beauty has usurped it from the young. But if there is a costume, anyone can wear it, anyone can be feminine, including the erotically disenfranchised postmenopausal woman. It is not that she makes femininity ugly but, rather, that she refuses to accept the exclusive canon of womanly beauty. Her defiance both shatters and expands the aesthetic of femininity and opens the way to new meanings of woman.

One of my friends wears her hair in a braid that reaches the middle of her back. She used to ask me, "Do I look old and severe like this?" I'd look at her hair, which is whiter each time I see her, once or twice a year, and the lines in her face, the creamy peach or subtle pink lipstick, the lavender, apricot, or buff eyeshadow, and her radiant complexion, and I'd say, "You're beautiful." Now she no longer asks the question. "It suits me," she says of her hairstyle and adds, "Fuck 'em."

Carolyn Heilbrun writes,

> Biographers often find little overtly triumphant in the late years of a subject's life, once she has moved beyond the categories our available narratives have provided for women. Neither rocking on a porch, nor automatically offering her services as cook and housekeeper and child watcher, nor awaiting another chapter in the heterosexual plot, the old woman must be glimpsed through all her disguises which seem to preclude her right to be called woman. She may well for the first time be woman herself.[6]

I am not promoting femininity but, rather, its fluidity. Even though femininity is misogyny's attempt to sanitize the female body, femininity is also a complex of pleasures that are lived and available and that women can use in order to change them. The heterosexual plot may try to entrap old(er) women in youth, the purchase of beauty products, plastic surgery, and gym memberships, but age triumphs over youth and cannot be contained by purchases or by the fictions in outworn biographical narratives. Postmenopausal eroticism, which includes taking pleasure in the vision of oneself and creating that pleasure, is overt triumph over societal and self-repulsion.

Women can choose dyed hair, red lipstick, "inappropriate" dress, styles of flamboyance, spectacle, elegance, or "tastelessness" that may be indicators of self-love and lust for living. Margaret Simons recounts her first sight of Simone de Beauvoir: "I was shocked when she opened the door. In spite of looking old and wrinkled, she had the audacity to wear red lipstick and bright red nail polish!"[7] In this context the word *audacity* seems ageist. Although I like the implication or effect of red's rudeness, the idea that an old(er) woman must be brave to wear bright cosmetics saddens me. Color is pleasure, and Simons's shock suggests partial recoil. A viewer cannot assume that an old(er) woman alive with colors and sensuous bodily and clothing surfaces is trying to mask her age because she hates herself.[8] Then the narrative closes. The old(er) woman who chooses pleasure does not wait for the next chapter, which patriarchy has already written. The heterosexual plot, having excluded old(er) women from the love story of romance and breeding, has no words for women's love of themselves.

My mother dyes her hair bird's-wing black, and she wears crimson lipstick. After almost forty years of cutting her hair very short, she's growing it, at age 81.

My father tells her she has a heartshaped face.

[*Frueh's voice becomes soft and especially smooth.*]

My mother is the face of love.

Well-preserved does not describe mom or grandma, my cosmetologist or my friend, for femininity has not mummified them. To preserve is to protect, to save from spoilage or rotting, to keep for future use, to maintain an area for hunting, to put up fruit. The well-preserved old(er) woman is always in danger of becoming overripe, damaged by age, unsavable and unsavory, worthless for the mating chase because she is a victim of language whose hatred of her rigidifies pleasure. The well-preserved woman is a dead body, embalmed by a disgusted secularization of women once the culturally sacred womb can no longer bear children.

The postmenopausal body deserves cultural resurrection as a site of love and pleasure.

Without love, there is no revolution,

And without pleasure, there is no freedom.

The Other Side of Privilege

Female pleasure has been theorized in terms of sexual difference but insufficiently in terms of women's differences from women. This matters, because patriarchy has determined reproductive woman to be desirable, a site of pleasure, and postreproductive woman to be undesirable. Younger women live the privilege of bondage to the eroticized reproductive ideal. Old(er) women live beyond that privilege.

The castrated woman of Freudian theory gains power, the phallus, by bearing a child. Her erotic power is beholden to insemination, imagined or real, and erotic myth builds on woman's capacity to seduce the male organ into the hole/hold of creation or to mangle male hopes. Man fears the cunt (*vagina dentata*), for it may destroy him, but he worships the womb, for it aggrandizes his self-image. This story lays the groundwork for hatred of old(er) women. A man cannot impregnate a postmenopausal woman, cannot even imagine his creativity visible in her body. Thus menopause is a subversion of female reproductive organs as the origin of male desire (and greed), of erotic symbols and narratives, and of womanhood when spiritualized as cosmic center of the female body.[9]

Womb-privilege operates along with the eroticization of young(er), firm(er) flesh and muscles, which represent the phallic symbol, the penis, in its state of power, erection. The old(er) body is the equivalent of detumescence and represents phallic failure. So man must avoid entry into the tomb of his desire.

Womb is a privileged word, whereas *uterus* is not used in a spiritual or romantic context. Menopausal and postmenopausal hysterectomies remove the uterus, not the womb. Elinor Gadon writes, "I suggest that women's wombs are their power centers, not just symbolically but in physical fact. When we say we act from our guts, from our deepest instincts, this is what we are speaking of. The power of our womb has been taken from us."[10] She is not talking about hysterectomy but, rather, of the devaluation of soul-and-mind-inseparable-from-the-body wisdom.

I agree that the body, woman's and man's, is a vehicle and site of wisdom, and perhaps Gadon's old(er) woman could retain her wiseblood regardless of whether she had a uterus. In *Privilege* (1990), filmmaker Yvonne Rainer presents the information that "by age 50, 31% of U.S. women will have had a hysterectomy. Hysterectomy is the most frequently performed operation in the U.S. . . . Hysterectomies . . . garner $800 million a year in gynecological fees. There is a popular saying among gynecologists that there is no ovary so healthy that it is not better removed, and no testes so diseased that they should not be left intact." I question the wisdom of locating female power—erotic, mystic, intuitive—in an organ that reads differently according to its owner's or former owner's age.

Luce Irigaray's "Ce Sexe qui n'en est pas un," as title, pun, and article, poeticizes and analyzes female pleasure as multiple, a polyvocality of organs, surfaces, sensations, and as inclusive of differences among women. I gather from Irigaray's arguments and ecstasies that any and all female bodies are erotic. Patriarchy, then, is arbitrary in its eroticization of the firm(er) phallic body, the vagina that is the corresponding nothing to man's something, the womb that is his dream of himself, and in so doing more severely castrates the old(er) woman than the young(er).

Arbitrariness is historically specific, so if Cranach's, Rubens's, Titian's, Renoir's, Boucher's, and Modigliani's nudes, all young but variously fleshed, have been seen as erotic, so can the old(er) female body. For the eye is polymorphously perverse and can be trained and lured into diverse pleasures, just as the libido can be.[11] Erotic desire floats, ready for grounding, awaiting direction from a desiring or loving subject. Changing the image of female erotic object from the youth ideal of Western art and advertising demands a change in the parameters and focus of love, the applications of femininity, and the source of female privilege, which has been patriarchy's maintenance of its own empire of desire that has used the female body to further male ends. In actuality, pleasures can abound in any body and therefore appear on "the other side of privilege."[12]

Rainer's *Privilege* presents variously privileged voices and characters, female, bourgeois, African-American, Nuyorican, male, poor, lesbian, heterosexual, young, menopausal, and postmenopausal. The last two positions receive the greatest attention and are spoken by a number of women and in diverse visual and narrative contexts. One story appears on a computer screen, and part of it reads:

> A woman who is just entering menopause meets a man at a conference at the University of El Paso. They hit it off. Later, after hearing his lascivious remarks about a much younger woman, she is shocked at having misinterpreted what she had thought was mutual sexual attraction. Toward evening, from the hilltop heights of the university, a Mexican-American student points out to her the sprawling shanties of Juárez across the Rio Grande. In the gathering dusk she realizes she is on two frontiers: Economically, she is on the advantaged side

> overlooking a third-world country. And sexually, having passed the frontier of attractiveness to men, she is now on the *other side* of privilege.

This declaration of self-recognition stuns me. I see a European-American woman of independence, self-esteem, professional standing, more than adequate income, and confidence in her attractiveness shocked to be persuaded that she is other from the self and persona she believed in. I see her standing above the Rio Grande, dumbstruck and fucked by a society in which, just as suddenly, women of fifty or so wake up to find that men have been the locus of their existence and to ask, now that they have fallen from the grace of womb-love, what do they love in themselves and in their unbecomingly hypervisible because erotically invisible sisters? In *Privilege,* Jenny, the menopausal hub figure, starts up from the bed where she has just had sex with a male lover, who is young in this flashback where she is her contemporary fiftyish self, and she exclaims, "My biggest shock in reaching middle age was the realization that men's desire for me was the lynchpin of my identity."

The El Paso story and the images it creates in my mind haunt me and force rumination. They point out a gap in women's lives and in the stories about them that begs to be filled by an eros that is self-reliant and resilient. The El Paso story speaks of loss and of the silence of teller and audience at the end of a sad or amazing tale. But to maintain that silence would be to accept the closure provided—dictated—by Heilbrun's heterosexual plot. So I continue the story and say that, loosened from the privilege of constrained eros, an old(er) woman adventures after different pleasures, polymorphous and perverse because they neither play to nor rant at the father who demands erotic conformity and submission and therefore provokes hostility, and because they demonstrate the impropriety of existing at all and the intractability of a subject who will not nullify her lust for living.

Grant Kester's discussion of alternative art's rant genre, practiced in large part by performance artists, including postfeminists, started me thinking about the rant nature of much visual art by postfeminists and post-postfeminists, exemplified in works by many young(er) women in *1920: The Subtlety of Subversion, the Continuity of Intervention* at the New York Gallery Exit Art/The First World (6 March–7 April 1993). Kester writes, "The implied viewer . . . is often a mythical father figure conjured up out of the artist's imagination to be shouted at, attacked, radicalized, or otherwise transformed by the work."[13] I believe the old(er) woman artist of feminist conscience speaks to the world, not to the father. When she taps into the polymorphously perverse libido, she can circumvent—and demolish—people's domination by the father-in-the-brain who oversees and de-eroticizes most bodies.

Awakening is a passage (El Paso, The Pass) on the great river (Rio Grande) of life, after which women can no longer pass for young. Passage releases them from the social order's dominant erotic games of coercive femininity and heterosexuality, and conscious passage encourages new formulations of desire. The proliferation of polymorphous perversities from and within the postmenopausal soul-and-mind-inseparable-from-the-body open-ends female ways of seeing and being pleasure. The old(er) woman need not be the Crone or the matron or feminine forever, ways of aging that satisfy some women but are insufficiently diverse. The Crone archetype offers a model of wise old age, usually earth-connected; the matron is a model of self-sufficiency and welcome invisibility; and feminine forever may necessitate posthuman control—cosmetic surgery and hormone replacement therapy.[14]

The social order is safer with fewer models than with many and is especially secure when women mourn their youth. They mourn because they see so few models of power and pleasure. The proliferation of polymorphous perversities in postmenopausal women's self-presentation and -concept would help reify historian and singer Bernice Reagon's statement about menopause, and I paraphrase her, It's the point from which you fly.[15]

The Art of Flying

Visual art reifies pleasure. Images, objects, and artmaking processes are testimonies to artmaking as the production of pleasure, for the artist and for the viewer. Making art is the practice of love, and many women artists over fifty say that doing what you love keeps you young. Underlying the various ways women express belief in artmaking as fountain of youth, I find erotic motivation.

The erotic is rich living and, ultimately, an involvement in the transformation of self and society. The erotic is pleasure-work, the means and ends of flight. Its practitioner engages in social risk and provides social sanctuary, for the art of flying is a provident skill. I think of Erica

Jong's *Fear of Flying* (1973), about a young(er) woman's investment in erotic action and fantasy—the Zipless Fuck—and compare the novel with *Privilege*, in which Jenny finds that men have flown, and I imagine she must search out new ways to fly, not necessarily without men but definitely different from a young(er) woman's assertions of erotic will.[16] Jenny exemplifies Maxine Kumin's Sleeping Beauty:

> When Sleeping Beauty wakes up
> she is almost fifty years old.[17]

The rude awakening is the beginning of mature yet strangely fledgling flight, of a new erotic movement and new aesthetic assessments that do not demean Awakening Beauty for either the phobic dreams of old(er) women's age she has shared with patriarchy or for innocence about the mysterious beauty that has become aware of itself and that she must investigate. Sleeping Beauty wakes herself up from the coma of delivery by man, and though her prince may come, erotic union with him will not fit into the heterosexual plot. One reason is that she has negotiated an autoerotic awakening. Beauty Aroused is an erotic agent, Dorothy Sayers's "advanced old woman [who] is uncontrollable by any earthly force," for she can fly.[18]

A number of women artists over fifty are overcoming Sleeping Beauty's fear of flying. Below I discuss the work of three: Bailey Doogan, Claire Prussian, and Carolee Schneemann.[19] Each formulates a reification of the aging physical and psychic body, a way to see and experience sensation, emotion, and palpability, to understand erotic accesses and outlets of the self, whose wholeness an individual, looking at or touching her body, cannot entirely grasp.

Beauty Aroused is pleasure-vehicle, the artist, and pleasure-product, the art. Beauty Aroused is subject, muse, and artist in service of her self, a triune power whose erotic engagement in visual and female (self-) pleasure dismantles Diana Vreeland's misogynistic, Paglian statement that opens this paper: "The beauty of painting, of literature, of music, of *love* . . . this is what men have given the world, not women."

I do not want the listener to think that just because Doogan, Prussian, and Schneemann all deal with the female body I am reducing visual pleasure in women's art to anatomical or somatic expression. Visual pleasure, and its relationship with female pleasure, continues to be a largely unarticulated aspect of feminist discourse. I attribute that partly to the lingering success of Laura Mulvey's "Visual Pleasure and

Narrative Cinema" (see note 5, below) and partly to feminists' body-phobia, even prudery, this despite a growing literature on the body.

Theoretical focus on the female body as site and vehicle of feminist visual pleasure is necessary. CORP (Canadian Organization for the Rights of Prostitutes), addressing what they considered feminists' condescending and patronizing attitude toward prostitutes, wondered in a 1987 publication, "How can they [feminists] hear us talk, how can they hear us when they can't even hear their own bodies? They are continually shaping it with their minds. . . . Whatever their bodies are telling them somehow comes up through their minds, and then they shape what's comfortable."[20] I would rather have a shapely soul-and-mind-inseparable-from-the-body, disciplined, determined, and liberated by inevitable discomforts of thinking and feeling, than be shaped by intellectual prudence bordering on a prudery that disjoints mind from soul from body and sex from intellect.

For better or worse, we are wed in utero to our bodies, and as my friend Helen says about the body, "It's all we have." This is more realistic than fatalistic. The body is radical, is, in tandem with mind, root and heart of knowing. A woman's sexual organs do not define her root-heart, for that would mean the rest of her is aphasic. Beauty Aroused is erotic art(ist), fighter, speaker, and seer militating against continuing Cartesian escapism into presence through mind. Beauty Aroused minds the body and embodies thought—she is an activist—and she reifies the fact that woman is an erotic territory yet to be explored by herself. That exploration is necessary and revolutionary. If you think it is utopian, consider that eros is reality rather than perfection, and always within reach.

Bailey Doogan

Doogan says, "Female pleasure is a Pandora's box. So much goes against your realizing what female pleasure is, but something about female pleasure is connected with a freedom and acceptance of myself. I find that I often can't talk about the things I care about and the passion for what I care about is reserved for my work.

"I feel more of a going inward as I get older," and perhaps this is associated with a positively narcissistic scrutiny: "The older I get the more I stare at myself." This desire to know one's soul-inseparable-from-the-body through observation is Doogan-the-artist's pleasure, and she duplicates her visual self-fascination in her paintings of the old(er) female nude. She says, "I feel as if I'm crawling over the bodies inch by inch" as she paints.[21]

Doogan wants to "define the body in relation to culture." As a painter of the female nude/herself seen in her model's flesh, Doogan uses male visual language to shatter it while simultaneously creating what male visual language has made absent. Feminists have continually reiterated the problem of producing changed meanings while speaking male language, which has been the only one available. Don't vocabulary—the female body—and syntax—youth and beauty—wrest change from the female and feminist painter's hands? Mightn't an aging body simply be perceived or interpreted as a facile mockery of the standard? No, for the old(er) body, in contemporary American culture, is never a gloss. The old(er) body, within the conventions of Western art and its vampiric relative, contemporary advertising, represents chaos, because it does not submit to the strictures of domination that have pictured the female body for man's eyes. While the standard female nude or nearly nude in advertising is a sweet that pains a woman's mind-and-soul-inseparable-from-the-body, Doogan's figures in works such as *Mea Corpa* (1992) and *Mass* (1991) are sights for women's sore eyes.

Whereas the conventional female nude is an icon of womb-worship, Doogan's nudes retheorize the canonical female body.[22] Her iconoclasm goes beyond resistance or rejection because she invents a difference from the norm that does not transcend the significance of liminal experience. Although Western culture has construed the female body to be more liminal than the male, because the former manifests blood mysteries and has culturally been defined more cruelly than the male body as exemplar of time's ravaging passage, Western art has denied that liminality by shunning age (as well as pregnancy, menstruation, and menopause).[23] Western art's use of the female body to control time—aging and death—contributes to our fear of flesh that moves, wrinkling, even shrinking, with age in a dephallicizing process.[24] As I said earlier, the old(er) female body is the tomb of man's desire. To picture the old(er) female nude is to represent the ultimate patriarchal taboo, the end of patriarchy. Doogan's female nudes, then, are models of feminist and female pleasure. They are made by a woman who questions to death the premises of erotic argument (only the young(er) body is desirable, and patriarchy decides that), and the subject who questions experiences pleasure.

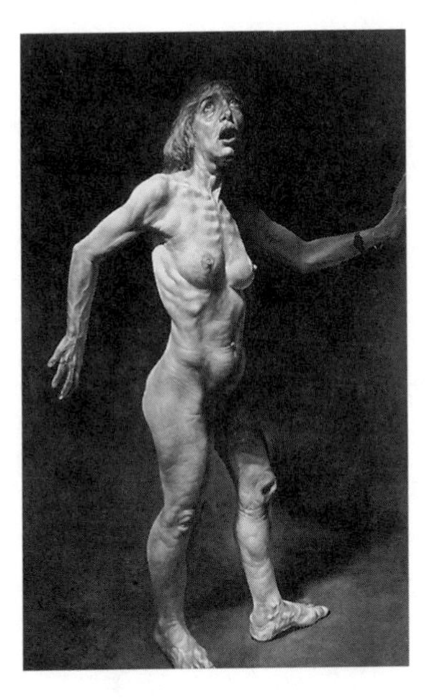

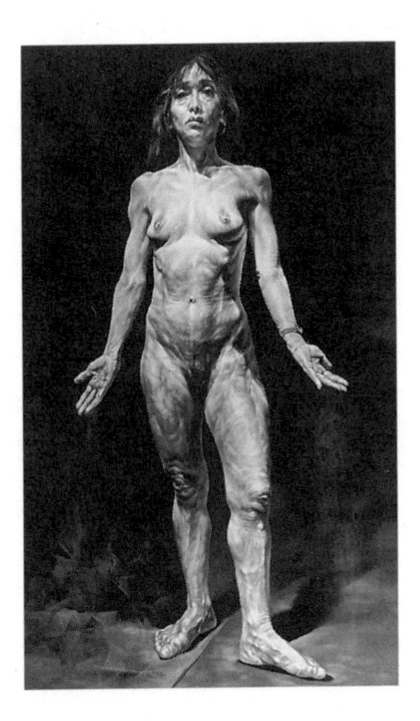

The liminal body, Sleeping Beauty, represents desire.

[*Frueh says, "Lights down, please. Projector on." A slide of* Mea Corpa *appears. As the discussion of the painting progresses, Frueh shows details so that the audience cannot ignore its departures from conventional nude beauty.*]

She is *Mea Corpa, my* body, standing in the posture of the resurrected Christ, and her flesh moves with the energy of eros. Veins protrude along her calves and feet, skin creases at her ankles and waist and both clings to and bulges at her knees. Light does not caress her, it illuminates her new seductions: heavy eyelids and undereye pouches, bony shoulders, muscled arms and legs worked out in the gym and worked on by the force of gravity over time. Doogan's crawling over every inch results in a body that feels like fluids, flesh, and organs and that recalls Monique Wittig's resuscitation of the female body in *The Lesbian Body:*

> THE PLEXUS THE GLANDS THE
> GANGLIA THE LOBES THE
> MUCOSAE THE TISSUES THE
> CALLOSITIES THE BONES THE
> CARTILAGE THE OSTEOID THE
> CARIES THE MATTER THE MARROW
> THE FAT THE PHOSPHORUS THE

> MERCURY THE CALCIUM THE
> GLUCOSES THE IODINE THE
> ORGANS THE BRAIN THE HEART
> THE LIVER THE VISCERA THE
> VULVA THE MYCOSES THE
> FERMENTATIONS THE VILLOSITIES
> THE DECAY THE NAILS THE TEETH
> THE HAIRS THE HAIR THE SKIN
> THE PORES THE SQUAMES THE
> PELLICULES THE SCURF THE SPOTS[25]

It is not that Doogan shows everything, and Wittig's words are certainly neither enumeration nor description. Like Wittig, Doogan expresses flux and inseparability by using erotic syntax and creating a body—a word that feels too categorical in Doogan's and Wittig's usages—that deserves the name "m/y radiant one."[26]

Naked splendor in *Mea Corpa* offers itself to female eyes and recovers itself from the guilt, mea culpa, of not being beautiful or correct enough to be seen. This female figure steps out of the (literal) darkness (of guilt) deaccessorized of conventional erotic props such as bed, fan, drapery, fruit, flowers. She displays appetite for herself, *my body,* not the one Western art invented and permuted for Woman, so *my body* has risen, flown from the dystopian eros developed by patriarchy. Doogan puts an end to anorexia of the spirit.

In 1987, at forty-six, Doogan painted *Femaelstrom,*

[*slide appears*]

in which a female St. Sebastian, haloed in gold leaf and pierced by arrows—actual sticks of wood dipped in red paint—gazes towards a bevy of bean pods, upon each of which Doogan has painted a young bikinied woman. The femaelstrom is women's confusion over Western culture's splitting of woman into saint and sinner. The next year Doogan produced a monumental triptych, *RIB (Angry Aging Bitch),*

[*slide appears*]

a mixed-media drawing that rails against woman's creation from the body-mind of man. In each of the piece's panels Doogan depicts an old(er) female nude. *Femaelstrom* and *RIB* are characteristic of Doogan's late 1980s female nude—suffering, melancholy, aging in monumental resoluteness and inspirational rage. The nude in *Mea Corpa, Mass,*

[*slide appears*]

and *Hairledge* (1993), all completed after Doogan turned fifty, suggests reconciliation, the balance in one body of sensuousness and spirituality, a redirection of displeasures from injuries sustained from the fathers to pleasures maintained in service to oneself.

Pleasure, like beauty, is in the eye of the beholder, who is me and you and who may wish to remake the meaning of Pandora's box. Remember Doogan's "Female pleasure is a Pandora's box." Female pleasure curses only misogynists, and we need not believe Hesiod's story that Pandora's box held evils and afflictions, that, though warned not to open it, she did out of curiosity, and consequently made humankind accursed. The "curse" of the old(er) female body is chaos. The culture that has perceived and mythicized the old(er) female body's terrific disorderliness has also made it unsightly and invisible in order to shore up the young(er) female body as an object and idea of phallic security. When the old(er) woman, Doogan in this case, releases her polymorphously perverse libido, she releases chaos, which is Pandora's gift.[27]

Doogan's female nude is vessel, locus, and outpouring of curiosity and subjectivity. The name Pandora means All-giver, from the Greek *pan*, all, and *dōron*, gift. Barbara Walker writes, "Pandora's vessel was . . . a honey-vase, *pithos,* from which she poured out blessings: a womb-symbol like the Cornucopia."[28] So that we do not continue the womb-worship that is detrimental to old(er) women's erotic social security, let us simply say that Pandoras, such as Doogan, dying for a look into what man has warned them in visual and popular images not to see, release self-knowledge, which is a blessing.

Pandora's box holds erotic sweets, which patriarchy withholds from old(er) women, whose defiance is auto-expression, without which transformation, social or personal, cannot occur. To turn Doogan's phrase, Pandora's box is female pleasure gone wild, the pandemonium feared by some viewers of Doogan's paintings and blessed by others. I've heard several people compare her figures to Ivan Albright's. Both artists do present unforgiving scrutinies, but Albright's most-remembered paintings depict pathetic specimens of decay. Their flesh mocks them with the futility not only of vanity but of living itself, so the figures, which are rarely nudes, become emblems of dying and death. Their skin looks iridescent, diseased, and worn, and they seem predisposed to growing tumors. If Doogan's bodies seem like sore sights that frighten women's eyes, that is only because they are unaccustomed to chaos, which is

Doogan's assertion of corporeal specificity and individuality as beautiful. Doogan is friendly to the female body, and *Mea Corpa,* in Doogan's language, reads most significantly as destigmatization, a transformation from guilt to self-possession that is responsible to women's real bodies. This happens because Doogan has made a spectacle out of the old(er) female body.[29]

[*blank slide*]

Claire Prussian

Claire Prussian writes to me, "I remembered when I was in art school how much more I loved drawing fat old models. Young ones were not interesting. Funny, I haven't thought about that in *years*. I love clothes *so* much more now, and jewelry. Beautiful things have assumed a different dimension, it's not just material. And I feel more comfortable in my body, spiritually—not physically—too many aches, pains, but I'd rather feel this way."[30]

In her studio Prussian talks with me about clothes and apologizes several times for her interest in them. Later, after having lunch at a restaurant in Chicago's Neiman Marcus Building, we look at clothes. She points out a Mary MacFadden gown that falls in rippling pleats from a densely sequined and embroidered bodice. Floor-length and long-sleeved, the dress would entirely cover a body. Prussian speaks of such dresses as armor. They would conceal a wearer in power. She says too that many old(er) women's hairdos are helmets. "If I have to be old," said Prussian at lunch, "I'll be the most elegant old woman you've ever seen." She adds, "Style doesn't take lots of money."

Prussian's interest in clothing and style must not be misconstrued as simplistically materialist. Although feminists heatedly critique the dogma of beauty, they have written very little about beauty itself.[31] Patriarchally instituted beauty doctrine—look young-sexy-beautiful so men can better worship your womb—garners so much feminist attention that feminist theories and practices of female beauty, especially regarding old(er) women, do not arise.

The feminist critical gaze has eyed Joan Collins and Madonna, professional beauties skilled in professional seductiveness.[32] Madonna and Alexis Carrington, an old(er) sexpot played by Collins in the nighttime soap opera *Dynasty,* function for some feminists as women who are self-consciously desiring and desirable: they are sexual agents as much as objects, and they enjoy both roles. Like Madonna and Alexis, Prussian can afford to buy glamor, but, unlike them, she does not adhere to the erotic orthodoxies of slenderness clothed in absolute fashionableness, skin made up into a doll-like dream, and signs of aging entirely eradicated by hair coloring or surgical and photographic means. Prussian underwent cosmetic surgery but directed her physician to leave certain lines because "I wanted to look my age but more rested." Prussian's love is not youth but style, which can be the creation of self, whereas fashion necessitates the bending of taste to currency.

Wherever possible, women must reinterpret beauty in their personal style, in their work and workplaces, so as to make beauty nongenerational. Women must control the images of their desire, which means making them anew. I don't expect absolute authenticity, images from the origin of female desire—can we know or believe in such a location?—but I do demand complexity in the symbolic representation of women. Beauty in old(er) women requires creative visual expression that burrows and flies with Naomi Wolf's idea in *The Beauty Myth: How Images of Beauty Are Used Against Women* that old(er) women are "darker, stronger, looser, tougher, sexier. The maturing of a woman who has continued to grow is a beautiful thing to behold."[33] But women must soar and dig much farther. Though Wolf's assertion is easy for young(er) women such as herself to pronounce, it is exceedingly difficult to practice from an old(er) body. Patriarchy's horror of the old(er) female body stems from attraction to the vision and then to embodiments of old(er) beauty, from fear of men's damnation by new desires that would mean oblivion, an end to the psychic perpetuation of control over women and to the actual perpetuation of the human race. Man would forget his duties.

Prussian's images of beauty for women sometimes rawly confront aging, but more often they displace it. The beauty of armor and helmet—the screen, to use Prussian's word, of style—appears repeatedly in her drawings, prints, and paintings. Screen should not be confused with fashion, for fashion shifts, it is a personality that flutters, while style holds, like a barrier invested with self.

Born in 1930, Prussian says that "growing old is a real loss of self, a narcissistic injury" that may result in "a dedication to screen." In her art the screen, which includes luxurious fabrics and settings, proliferation of pattern, reveling in flowers and plants, and sensuous detailing of aging skin, is the psychic body. Her images depart radically from cosmetic surgery, the *au courant,* posthuman way to screen, or mask, female aging. In contrast, Prussian's works are screens that let down a guard against aging. They both comfort the viewer and set her on edge.

Vanitas (1981)

[*slide appears*]

is a triptych whose rich lithographic tones describe the face of a woman about Prussian's age who was a friend. In the right panel she faces left, almost profiled; the central panel features her larger, head-on, and framed so that no hair shows; and in the left panel she is in three-quarters view, facing in. All the portraits are insistent closeups of a goddess of aging whose nonchalant sophistication—the way she holds a drink as if toasting or caresses one finger with another—speaks self-awareness. Prussian delineates her subject's fine and deep lines, eye pouches, and nose-to-lip folds. They are as lovingly and sensuously determined as are the hollows of her cheeks as she eyes the viewer from the central panel.

Vanitas treats the end of female vanity based in conventional femininity. Unlike Renaissance paintings whose theme is vanity, Prussian's print does not feature a young naked woman gazing in a mirror, nor does Prussian critique female "narcissism." Her composition recalls a three-part mirror, before which a woman makes up while looking at herself closely and at different angles. Here the making up is not cosmetic but, rather, a reconciliation with one's face by examining it.

In Latin *vanitas* means emptiness, and *vanitas* paintings in seventeenth-century Flanders and Holland were allegorical still lives. Prussian does not use any traditional objects from such paintings, which are meditations on transience and the emptiness of worldly possessions: an overturned bowl or cup refers literally to emptiness. Here the old(er) subject is herself the symbol of *vanitas*, for she represents the end of herself as (man's) worldly possession, the emptiness of that status. The emotion conveyed, however, is not emptiness, for *Vanitas* is starkly full, visually and otherwise. The woman's face fills each frame with determined resonance, and her glass isn't empty. In fact, she seems to toast herself and the viewer. She is Still Life, alive, visibly unavoidable.

In *Vanitas-Tas-Tas* (1988),

[*slide appears*]

Prussian photocopied the earlier piece in four multiples that descend from ten and one-half inches to a little more than five inches high and that stand behind one another, as if in embrace. She hinged each triptych like an altarpiece and decorated the outer altarpiece panels with brilliantly colored fake jewels glued onto patterned Japanese papers. Replication adds a funhouse dimension, an Alice in Wonderland perceptual distortion, which relates to women's conceptual self-distortions as they age: intimate knowledge of one's appearance becomes magnified and looms in one's mind, beauty seems false, only a layer of glitter. Prussian seems to take herself/the old(er) woman to task for her vanity—tas, tas sounds like tsk, tsk—but also delights in the adornment of the altarpieces. Each one is a gem of private and sacred scale, a dedication to the possibility of beauty-in-realism.

[*blank slide*]

Prussian loves her subjects and their environs, belongings, and gestures. Her fastidious, explicit way of looking, whether in photorealist drawings and prints or later faux-naïf paintings, reminds me of Chantal Akerman's words in a 1977 interview about her film *Jeanne Dielman* (1975):

> If you choose to show a woman's gestures so precisely, it is because you love them. In some way you recognize those gestures that have always been denied and ignored. I think the real problem with women's films has nothing to do with content. It's that hardly any women really have confidence enough to carry through on their feelings. Instead the content is the most simple and obvious thing. They deal with that and forget to look for formal ways to express what they are and what they want, their own rhythms, their own way of looking at things.[34]

Prussian sees and wants fullness, eros, age. She finds and plants her women in the midst of flowers. In the prismacolor drawings *Woman in Blue* and *Woman in Blue with Flowers* (both 1980),

[*slide appears*]

a gray-haired woman with crimson lips and nails and diamond heart pendant sits in front of a mass of flowers. Male poets and artists have equated women erotically with fruits and flowers: women blossom and wither; are succulent, then dry up. Flowers' aesthetic and sensual beauty, epitomized in the nineteenth century by Dante Gabriel Rossetti's visually and symbolically seductive use of them in relation to young(er) women, in Prussian's work calls into question the oppositional duality of youth and age, life and death. The subject in *Woman in Blue with Flowers* cocks her head, opens her voluptuous mouth in a near-sneer, moves her hands with the studied poise of a feminine smoker—her Tiparillo is caught in the breath of her conversation, in a pose that can no longer be read as flirtatious, for she is an uncanny queen of hearts. She covers her soul with sunglasses, but her body is soul nonetheless, a flower that shouts vitality. So does the body in *Still Life I,*

[*slide appears*]

a 1981–82 lithograph of an unclothed woman lying in an abundance of blooms—roses, irises, birds of paradise, and many more—that are her analog.

[*blank slide*]

The body becomes less relevant in a series of portraits from the early 1980s. Or perhaps I should say that the psychic body is obviously paramount in the material world that covers and surrounds the flesh. In such compositions the sitter is defined by a

[*slide of* Portrait of Grace Hokin *(1982) appears*]

deep-rose lace dress and a dusty pink and gray abstract floral patterned drape, or by her

[*slide of* Woman from New Jersey *(1983) appears*]

fluffy white cat, blond helmet hair, multicolored sweater, and literal screen of vegetation, or by her

[*slide of* Portrait of Shirley Cooper *(1982) appears*]

fur jacket and sofa of similarly delicate hues, or by a

[*slide of* Portrait of Ruth Nath *(1982) appears*]

soft apricot wing chair, butter-colored curtains, and forsythia sprays in a large rust-orange vase.

[*blank slide*]

In paintings from the mid-1980s to the present, *each thing*—flowers, fish, potted plants, wallpaper, mirrors reflecting the artist—possesses uncanny vitality. Often the mirrors and long, distorted perspectives push and open space into the super real—past, future, mythic, and strangely present times and places which are the psychic body. There the human face and figure are usually wistfully pathetic and undemanding of the eye. They are simply a visible part of the universe, and the psychic body shows its age in this displacement replete with complexity, timelessness, and beauty.

Kathleen Woodward theorizes a mirror stage of old age in *Aging and Its Discontents: Freud and Other Fictions,* and one section, based on Freud's writings, treats the uncanny, which may be an effect of looking into a mirror and recognizing, with shock and fright, that one is old. The familiar turns unfamiliar, for, according to Freud, the familiar has been repressed. He also relates the uncanny to castration anxiety, which may recall Prussian's belief that "growing old is a real loss of self, a narcissistic injury." The phallus dies and the double rises. Woodward says Freud follows Otto Rank in stating that in an early era of human history the double assured immortality and armed a person against death, but it came later to be seen as a messenger *of* death.[35]

Prussian sees herself over and over. In *Untitled* (1991),

[*slide appears*]

a triptych whose panels she displays diagonally, Prussian appears in a magnifying mirror in the uppermost section, like a sad, decapitated head, and in the center panel we see her in the magnifying mirror and in a horizontal bathroom glass that reflects a younger Prussian opening a door to the room behind. We also see her as the entering figure would, from the rear. *The Beauty Shop* (1991)

[*slide appears*]

is a Land-O-Lakes butter-carton illusion in which an image retreats seemingly ad infinitum. The beauty-shop mirror reflects Prussian, as does a mirror held by the hairdresser, and her image appears too in another mirror to the right of his station. An uncanny pattern—a wilderness of large, reaching, blue fern fronds—decorates the wall and chair. The latter is empty, for Prussian exists only in the mirrors and in the extreme patterning that is the psychic body or the presence of the repressed. She keeps the eye so busy with her array of fronds, rippling-grained floorboards, bricks in the buildings outside the window, and a plant whose serpentine stalks inch along the floor toward both the chair and the viewer that she staves off the death-harbinger double.

Pattern displaces anxiety; it creates much where there may all too soon be nothing and puts order into the unpredictability of life. Pattern is beautiful. One's double may mean death, but Prussian actually multiplies herself and opens psychic and physical space far beyond the confines of any particular room she depicts. Perhaps the multiple image is self-protection, like the statues of Egyptian pharaohs that housed the ka, the spirit/double after death, so that he or she would continue in the afterlife.

Prussian has used explicit ancient Egyptian imagery in her work. One example is *Three Frozen Images: Beginning, Middle, End* (1984),

[*slide appears*]

where she stands, elegantly gowned in green—color of the generative, the everlasting—in an interior that resembles an Egyptian tomb. For the ancient Egyptians death was not the end, and for Prussian this tomb may be a house of life. Her back to us, she faces an altarpiece-like mirror and views herself in triple deity. Prussian says of daily life, "I want to see something gorgeous when I look in the mirror," so she cares about jewelry, beautiful makeup, the coordination of colors and fabrics. Rather than seeing Prussian's self-mirroring in her body of work as the fascination of "adaptive repulsion," in which the mirror distances one from oneself, we should understand Prussian's self-observation as amatory. The mirror in *Three Frozen Images* reflects the gorgeous self from more than one side, and the mirror can also be seen as a painting that, like a ka statue, keeps alive, provides nourishment for, the gorgeous spirit/double in the present.

[*blank slide*]

In the infant mirror stage the subject falls in love with herself, but if in the old(er) age mirror stage the observer identifies with her image, she is differently transformed, supposedly because she does not, cannot desire what she sees.[36] So she is set reeling away from herself. Prussian says there are things she does not enjoy about growing old—the loss of friends and family, "too many aches, pains." But her spiritual comfort leads her to say, "I'd rather feel this way" than young(er). In her art Prussian looks into, not at, the mirror. She does not deflect aging, for she desires the looking into herself, which is the look of love. Prussian loves the time spent in her studio more than any other: "It's the only place where time feels right, not too fast or too slow." The pleasures met and created in that kind of time appear in Prussian's libidinally invested representations.

Carolee Schneemann

Schneemann talks about "the ecstatic body and the power of the ecstatic. Sexual pleasure is a capacity and gift of the organism." Eros has consistently been both source and content of Schneemann's art. Probing, exposing, and loving a "hand-touch sensibility" while believing that "tactility is suspect" in Western culture, she continues to divest the female body of iconicity and to create "a *jouissance* beyond the phallus." This is a courageous project, for, as Schneemann says, androcentric culture has a "terror of the nonerect self"; it is age- and vulva-phobic. "The old woman is the ultimate betrayal of masculine imagination, the imagined ideal of the feminine," she says.[37] The old(er) body's tactility is especially threatening, for it is flesh that has moved by virtue of having been around so long; it is sliding, sinking, ever more earthbound. Testicles and penises move, but they belong to a reproductive program of male creation/creativity, and a penis can defy gravity. Young(er) breasts and labia move, but they are part of the reproductive plan and the heterosexual plot. Culture conceives of them as plush organs that time destroys: breasts sag, vaginas atrophy, and both dry up.[38] The realities of some men's impotence and some women's moist vaginas do not conform to cultural myth. At fifty-two one postmenopausal artist says, "I'm as horny as ever, and when I make love I'm as wet as ever."[39] Schneemann speaks of the possibility that "in the ancient goddess-worshipping cultures—Minoan, Sumerian, Celtic—there was a full female erotics, older women had respect, and men were their acolytes."[40]

Schneemann has certainly been interested in flesh, but as a vehicle rather than an end point of eros. Her classic performance *Meat Joy* (1964)

[*slide appears*]

was flesh that moves, an orgiastic

[*another slide of* Meat Joy *appears*]

dance of semi-clothed bodies and animal parts, an Aphroditean ritual. (She says that Dionysus stole orgiastic pleasures from Aphrodite.) While Schneemann has used her own classically beautiful body

[*slide of* Eye Body *(1963) appears*]

in her art—one artist says, "Carolee, she personifies the goddess each time she steps out in performance"—the intention has not been to make herself into an icon.[41] Carolee-as-goddess is not Womb-Worshipped One, patriarchy's docile deity, for she celebrates the female body for the pleasure of women. "In some sense I made a gift of my body to other women: giving our bodies back to ourselves."[42]

[*blank slide*]

In order to divest the female body of the iconicity that adheres to it through womb-worship and to counter, psychoanalytically speaking, its conversion into a phallic stand-in for (its lack of) male organs, Schneemann proves the existence of female organs. In *Interior Scroll* (1975)

[*slide appears showing sequential action*]

she stood naked and delicately unraveled from her vagina a ten-foot-long paper scroll folded in a "strange origami,"

[*blank slide*]

and in *Cycladic Imprints* (1988–92) she uses vulval images.[43] Like *Meat Joy*, *Cycladic Imprints* celebrates eros. For an artist of any age and sex this is a victory over cultural erotophobia, for an artist to continue such work over thirty years is a tribute to her faith and fortitude, and when a woman of fifty creates such work, it is a triumph over ageist assumptions about the pleasures and desires of old(er) women, and it diverges from the only archetype as yet provided for postmenopausal women, that of the Crone. I don't object to the Crone, for she is a figure of useful power and self-esteem for some women, but as one artist, who *is* a grandmother, said to me, "I'll never be the grandmother, I'll never be the Crone."[44]

Cycladic Imprints

[*slide appears*]

is an installation that embraces the viewer, who, upon entering, immediately absorbs and penetrates

[*another slide of* Cycladic Imprints]

a heady and sensual atmosphere of images, objects, sound, and dusky light. As she sits or walks

[*another slide of* Cycladic Imprints]

within a tangibility of eros, the viewer becomes the ecstatic body. Schneemann envelops the visitor in

[*another slide of* Cycladic Imprints]

a love potion, a tender orgy of slide projections—such as Cycladic statuettes, female nudes from art history, and

[*another slide of* Cycladic Imprints]

Schneemann's own vulva and torso, all beamed in dissolving relays from four positions—

[*another slide of* Cycladic Imprints]

sound, by Malcolm Goldstein, that flutters and hums into one's body like a wordless love song;

[*another slide of* Cycladic Imprints]

fifteen motorized violins, hung on and out from the walls, whose rhythmic movements suggest rhythms of sexual intercourse; and voluptuous,

[*another slide of* Cycladic Imprints]

linear abstractions of an hourglass or female form painted on the walls.

[*another slide of* Cycladic Imprints]

One's soul-and-mind-inseparable-from-the-body resonates to the overlay and transformation of images from historical, mythic, and (Schneemann's) personal memory, for *Cycladic Imprints* makes love.

[*another slide of* Cycladic Imprints]

In this installation the female body and its abstract figuration are everywhere, but they are not aestheticized in phallic terms and therefore are not conventional erotic models that say, "Look at me." Schneemann performs a feminist deaestheticization that recreates the female body in an intersubjective, in contrast to voyeuristic-phallic, mode. This is a restructuring of desire in which relationship is paramount. Such an artist/viewer interaction is mutuality, a subject to subject relationship that replaces the standard subject to art object one. This kind of interpenetration and embrace is mental and sensuous and, while it claims an individual's participation, it also permits her a singular though not separate presence within the spatial arena that is physical and psychic. The hand-touch sensibility reaches, caresses, and still leaves/makes room for the distance self-integrity requires.

Schneemann's visual and aural terms establish reciprocal space, where viewer and audience become absurd designations, for the gallerygoer is receptor, full of self, connections, and connectedness, but not receptacle, the feminine passive. Receptivity is *Cycladic Imprints*'s mode of communication. Images dissolve, music never forces entry, violins appear and disappear depending on light level and direction, so the piece is nondirective as to where a person might ground desire—except that grounding is clearly felt to be one's mind-and-soul-inseparable-from-the-body, both the organic and invisible sites of self and receptivity, onto and into which tones and images play.[45]

Schneemann does not create womb-space. She does focus on the female body, often as metonymic vulval form—the wall abstractions, violins and their cases, and, of course, her own organs. Historical repetition is the point, to which Schneemann has brought her partner in art and pleasure, the gallerygoer, as if through steady, continual orgasm, the kind a woman can undeliberately experience simply by sitting legs crossed and not moving, upper thighs slightly pressing at an unconscious angle. This is a leisurely route to pleasure which never has to peak. To read *Cycladic Imprints* as essentialist—vulva is woman's center, the transhistorical and cultural mark of Woman that marks her fate; Anatomy is Destiny—is to gloss over *Cycladic Imprints*'s intersubjectivity as theoretical proposition.[46] Here the vulva functions neither as a simplistic reversal of phallus as symbolic representation of desire nor as a facile glorification of the female body and its anatomical difference. *Cycladic Imprints* is not about woman's capacity to attract or to be fertile or to bear children. It is (about) female pleasure as historical resonance and present reality.

In *Cycladic Imprints* the (grand)mothers come.

[*blank slide. Frueh says, "Lights up, please."*]

Angela Carter writes in *The Sadeian Woman* that "Mother must never be allowed to come, and so to come alive." The (grand)mothers' pleasure is taboo. The expletive *motherfucker* identifies its object as pariah, curses him into place outside socialized sexual behavior. Schneemann dares and entices the participant lovingly to know the (grand)mothers' genitals, despised when not altogether obliterated.[47]

Taboo intimidates—and excites.

Schneemann's love opens a largely unmodeled articulation of female pleasure. In *Hard Core: Power, Pleasure, and the "Frenzy of the Visible,"* Linda Williams argues that porn films have looked for the truth—and difference—of women's pleasure, visually investigating the female body and probing it for confessions of pleasure, visible signs.[48] This is far more difficult to accomplish with the female than with the male body, which—reductive and often silly though the images are—can be shown with an erect or ejaculating penis as a sign of pleasure. Just as the conventional female nude is to a great degree a sign of male pleasure and thus of the invisibility of female pleasure—in terms of actively showing female pleasure or showing active female pleasure—porn, still a male-dominant field in regard to decision-making, has not made visible the anatomically hidden location of female pleasure. A shot of a clitoris, for instance, does not convey the sensation felt there. Porn can show the effects of female sexual pleasure in facial expressions and body gestures, but picturing cannot frame and measure female orgasm as it can—however inadequately—male orgasm. Visual examination of naked pleasure, the (idealized) female body—the skin, hair, and contours of the nude, the sex parts of the porn model or actress—cannot reveal the immeasurable. That model of pleasure-proof does not work. *Cycladic Imprints*, however, offers a different model, as explicit as porn when understood.

Barbara Hepworth, speaking as a sculptor who is a woman relating to form, says the relationship is a kind "of being rather than observing."[49] Observation can be a mode of surveillance and supremacy, the eye pinning and strutting over a sight. Being-in-relation treats the sight unseen. We move from I've got you in my sights, under the fascist control of one model of pleasure, to I've got you under my skin, where the irritant that is pleasure allows me room to move.

Without Love There Is No Revolution

Love is not a romance novel, and, contrary to Diana Vreeland's remark, neither is it a beauty that only men have created. Romance can be risk, adventure, and vision, in real terms that develop new narratives, which are old(er) women's love stories. The myth of the artist as risktaker, adventurer, and visionary is embedded in art history's and criticism's language of war and language of miracles, which are metaphors of spiritual and heroic prowess. Postmodern critiques have challenged that myth. But it doesn't die. Robert Mapplethorpe and David Wojnarowicz live on in contemporary art lore as heroes whose art and lives held erotic value, and the art press has lionized Matthew Barney, Richard Prince, Jeff Koons, and David Salle, still living exemplars of a masculine ethos, enforcers in their art of the patriarchal plot. Art history's and criticism's romance with them all is a nostalgic replay of Western cultural legends in current and easy incarnations of Joseph Campbell's Hero with a Thousand Faces.

When love is a large hunger for flesh that moves, the terms of romance transform. The art hero with the same old face turns into an actual old(er) woman whose art is known to provide erotic sustenance and activate ever more polymorphous perversities.

Notes

Work on this paper was supported by a Faculty Research Award from the University of Nevada, Reno. I especially appreciate the travel funds that allowed me to interview artists across the United States. My deep thanks go to the artists, for their time, honesty, and interest in this project.

Parts of this chapter appeared in M/E/A/N/I/N/G 14 *(November* 1993*) and are reprinted by permission of* M/E/A/N/I/N/G : A Journal of Contemporary Art Issues.

Other versions of "Polymorphous Perversities" have been delivered at:
The University of Arizona, Tucson, Arizona, June 1993
Art Works Gallery, San Jose, California, July 1993
Artemisia Gallery, Chicago, Illinois, October 1993
School of the Art Institute of Chicago, Chicago, Illinois, February 1994
Women in Photography Conference, Houston, Texas, March 1994

1. Angela Carter, *The Sadeian Woman and the Ideology of Pornography* (New York: Pantheon, 1978), 150, and Diana Vreeland, *D. V.*, ed. George Plimpton and Christopher Hemphill (New York: Alfred A. Knopf, 1984), 94.
2. I choose fifty because it is the median age at which menopause occurs for Western women and because menopause remains a powerful marker of aging. From June 1992 through January 1993 I sent questionnaires to one hundred women visual artists throughout the United States and interviewed women artists who deal with aging or the body in their work. Sixty-one people responded to the questionnaire, and all subjects were fifty or older. Key feminist writings on the erotic and female pleasure were published in the 1970s. They include Carter, *The Sadeian Woman;* Hélène Cixous, "Le Rire de la méduse," *L'Arc* 61 (1975): 39–54; Luce Irigaray, *Ce Sexe qui n'en est pas un* (Paris: Minuit, 1977); Audre Lorde, "Uses of the Erotic: The Erotic as Power," *Sister Outsider* (Trumansburg, New York: Crossing Press, 1984), 53–59; and Monique Wittig, *The Lesbian Body*, trans. David Le Vay (New York: Avon, 1975). In this paper I have used the following translations: Hélène Cixous, "The Laugh of the Medusa," trans. Keith Cohen and Paula Cohen, in Elaine Marks and Isabelle de Courtivron, eds., *New French Feminisms: An Anthology* (New York: Schocken, 1981), 245–64, and Luce Irigaray, "This Sex Which Is Not One," trans. Claudia Reeder, in Marks and de Courtivron, eds., *New French Feminisms*, 99–106.
3. Kathleen Woodward, *Aging and Its Discontents: Freud and Other Fictions* (Bloomington: Indiana University Press, 1991), 71.
4. Woodward, *Aging and Its Discontents*, 16, writes, "In Western culture age takes precedence over and may swallow up gender."
5. Laura Mulvey's classic essay "Visual Pleasure and Narrative Cinema," *Screen* 16 (Autumn 1975): 6–18, tells the reader, "It is said that analyzing pleasure, or beauty, destroys it. That is the intention of this essay. The satisfaction and reinforcement of the ego that represent the high point of film history hitherto must be attacked; not in favor of a reconstructed new pleasure, which cannot exist in the abstract, or of intellectualized unpleasure, but to make way for a total negation of the ease and plenitude of the narrative fiction film. The alternative is the thrill that comes from leaving the past behind without rejecting it, transcending outworn or oppressive forms, or daring to break with normal pleasurable expectations in order to conceive a new language of desire." Many feminists have used Mulvey's ideas to wage war against the male gaze that fixes woman as pleasure icon, and against the representation of the female body.

These interdictions have served to stymie exploration down certain avenues of female (visual) pleasure. Fear of the male gaze, which gives the power of looking and of projecting desire only to men and to patriarchal-pleasure disciplines, such as film and advertising, that designate the female body as an object and a spectacle of sex, robs women of their own bodies, the enjoyment of looking at themselves and other women with aroused, loving eyes. Two recent alternatives to Mulvey are Lorraine Gamman and Margaret Marshment, eds., *The Female Gaze: Women as Viewers of Popular Culture* (Seattle: Real Comet Press, 1989), and Cassandra Langer, "Transgressing *Le Droit du Seigneur:* The Lesbian Feminist Defining Herself in Art History," in Joanna Frueh, Cassandra Langer, and Arlene Raven, eds., *New Feminist Criticism: Art, Identity, Action* (New York: HarperCollins, 1994).

6. Carolyn Heilbrun, *Writing a Woman's Life* (New York: W. W. Norton, 1988), 131.
7. Margaret Simons, "In Memoriam," *Yale French Studies* 72 (1986): 204.
8. Woodward, *Aging and Its Discontents*, 158–59, tells one story from anthropologist Michèle Dacher's and psychoanalyst Micheline Weinstein's *The Story of Louise: Old People in a Nursing Home*. The book gives psychoanalytic portraits of eight people who live in a French nursing home and focuses also on Louise, a seventy-two-year-old bistro habitué. She had platinum blonde hair; she downed liquor, sung loud, and exchanged obscenities with others; her lipstick was dark, applied beyond her mouth's contours; and she was physically dirty. Woodward writes, "The point of course is that Louise's ferocious excess was a sign of her desire—quite literally her erotic desire for a man named Jean—and a measure of her more general powerful investment in life. Her remarkable appetite and energy, her flamboyance, which had nothing to do with parody, drew these two younger women to her."
9. Carter, *The Sadeian Woman*, 108–9, writes with elegant sarcasm, "For men, to fuck is to have some arcane commerce with this place of ultimate privilege. . . . The womb is the earth and also the grave of being; it is the warm, moist, dark, inward, secret, forbidden, fleshly core of the unknowable labyrinth of our experience. . . . Only men are privileged to return, even if only partially and intermittently, to this place of fleshly extinction; and that is why they have a better grasp of eternity and abstract concepts than we do. They want it for themselves, of course. . . . This is the most sacred of all places. Women are sacred because they possess it."
10. Elinor Gadon, *The Once and Future Goddess: A Symbol for Our Time* (San Francisco: Harper and Row, 1989), 289.
11. Louise Kaplan, *Female Perversions: The Temptations of Emma Bovary* (New York: Anchor, 1991), 507–8, writes about the looseness of desire: "The nymphet, the skin surface of the body, the curving neck . . . are not intrinsically beautiful or exciting. . . . These potential objects of desire are not sexually exciting until someone invests them with erotic value and with fantasies of desire. Because human sexuality is more a matter of imagination and fantasy than of biology, nothing pertaining to our sexuality is predetermined. . . . It is no more human to experience erotic desire for a person than to invest a fetish object

with erotic desire. . . . This polymorphous sexuality of ours . . . protects individuals from complete domination by the social order."

12. I quote from Rainer's film *Privilege*. The next paragraph provides the context.
13. Grant Kester, "Rhetorical Questions: The Alternative Arts Sector and the Imaginary Public," *Afterimage* 20 (January 1993): 14.
14. I use the phrase "feminine forever" loosely, to describe practices or performances of femininity that continue postreproductively, parody, or otherwise manipulate conventional femininity. The phrase comes from Dr. Robert A. Wilson, *Feminine Forever* (New York: M. Evans, 1966), which offers misogynist misinformation about menopause. A few examples are: "The woman becomes the equivalent of a eunuch," "I have seen untreated women who had shriveled into caricatures of their former selves," and "No woman can be sure of escaping the horror of this living decay." "Serenity and Power," in Germaine Greer's *The Change: Women, Aging and the Menopause* (New York: Alfred A. Knopf, 1992), 363–87, positively and extensively treats the matron. Barbara Walker's *The Crone: Woman of Age, Wisdom, and Power* (San Francisco: Harper and Row, 1985) revives the Crone for contemporary use and contemplation.
15. Reagon briefly commented on menopause as a guest on the *MacNeill-Lehrer News Hour*, 20 January 1993.
16. After thinking about the art of flying, I remembered Cixous's paragraph on flying in "The Laugh of the Medusa," 258. I quote the last sentence: "They (*illes*) [women] go by, fly the coop, take pleasure in jumbling the order of space, in disorienting it, in changing around the furniture, dislocating things and values, breaking them all up, emptying structures, and turning propriety upside down."
17. Quoted in Heilbrun, *Writing a Woman's Life*, 60.
18. Quoted in ibid., 124.
19. Others over fifty who deal with aging, the female body, and/or female pleasure in their art are Anne Noggle, May Stevens, Ida Applebroog, Hannah Wilke (died 28 Janury 1993), Joan Semmel, Vera Klement, Rachel Rosenthal, Elise Mitchell Sanford, Nancy Spero, Louise Bourgeois, Charle Varble, Athena Tacha, Leila Daw, and Barbara Hammer (filmmaker).
20. "Realistic Feminists: An Interview with Valerie Scott, Peggy Miller, and Ryan Hotchkiss of the Canadian Organization for the Rights of Prostitutes (CORP)," in Laurie Bell, ed., *Good Girls/Bad Girls: Feminists and Sex Trade Workers Face to Face* (Seattle: Seal Press, 1987), 213.
21. All Doogan's statements were made during a telephone conversation with the author, 4 February 1993.
22. Doogan's nudes are "theoretical insofar as they investigate the very fundamentals of visuality, representation, and image construction." See Johanna Drucker, "Visual Pleasure: A Feminist Perspective," *M/E/A/N/I/N/G* 11 (May 1992): 8.
23. Gail Sheehy's "The Unspeakable Passage: Is There a Male Menopause?" *Vanity Fair* (April 1993): 164–67, 218–20, 222–27, may inspire sympathy for men's thinning hair, impotence, and sexual and professional insecurities.
24. See Joanna Frueh, "The Fear of Flesh That Moves," *High Performance* 14 (Fall 1991): 70–71, for a discussion of the dread and pleasures of bodily liminality.
25. Wittig, *The Lesbian Body*, 37.

26. Ibid., 159. In the introduction to *The Lesbian Body* Margaret Crosland quotes Wittig regarding her pronouns: "*J/e* is the symbol of the lived, rending experience which is *m/y* writing, of this cutting in two which throughout literature is the exercise of a language which does not constitute m/e as subject."
27. Lorraine O'Grady, "Olympia's Maid: Reclaiming Black Female Subjectivity," *Afterimage* 20 (Summer 1992): 14, articulates the black female body's construction as chaos in relation to the white female body. Her thinking helped me to understand the old(er) female body's construction as chaos in relation to the young(er) female body.
28. Barbara G. Walker, *The Woman's Encyclopedia of Myths and Secrets* (San Francisco: Harper and Row, 1983), 767.
29. For an extended analysis and interpretation of Doogan's work see Joanna Frueh, "Bailey Doogan: Reconciliation," *Artists of Conscience II*, exhibition catalogue (New York: Alternative Museum, 1992), 25–31.
30. Claire Prussian, undated letter received by the author in February 1993. All the following statements are taken from an interview with the author, 8 June 1992, Chicago.
31. Critiques include Wendy Chapkis, *Beauty Secrets: Women and the Politics of Appearance* (Boston: South End, 1986), Robin Tolmach Lakoff and Raquel L. Scherr, *Face Value: The Politics of Beauty* (Boston: Routledge and Kegan Paul, 1984), and Naomi Wolf, *The Beauty Myth: How Images of Beauty Are Used Against Women* (New York: Anchor, 1991).
32. See Belinda Budge, "Joan Collins and the Wilder Side of Women: Exploring Pleasure and Representation," and Shelagh Young, "Feminism and the Politics of Power: Whose Gaze Is It Anyway?" in Gamman and Marshment, *The Female Gaze*, 102–11, 173–88, for feminist considerations and conflicts about sex queens Madonna and Joan Collins.
33. Wolf, *The Beauty Myth*, 286.
34. Chantal Akerman quoted in Teresa de Lauretis, "Aesthetic and Feminist Theory: Rethinking Women's Cinema," in Arlene Raven, Cassandra Langer, and Joanna Frueh, eds., *Feminist Art Criticism: An Anthology* (New York: HarperCollins, 1991), 137. Originally published in *New German Critique* 34 (Winter 1985).
35. Woodward, *Aging and Its Discontents*, 63.
36. See ibid., 67, for a discussion of the mirror stage of old age.
37. Schneemann's words are from an interview with the author, 18 June 1992, New York, except for "hand-touch sensibility," which is from a text Schneemann read as part of the performance *Interior Scroll*, originally given in 1975, and "a *jouissance* beyond the phallus," which appears in Lisa Jardine's "The Politics of Impenetrability," in Teresa Brennan, ed., *Between Feminism and Psychoanalysis* (London: Routledge, 1989), 64.
38. Rosetta Reitz, *Menopause: A Positive Approach* (London: Penguin, 1977), 104–5, compiled a "Twinge List" of "words and phrases used to describe menopause and the menopausal woman." Cultural conceptions of menopause are currently undergoing revision, but attitudes in some of Reitz's list, pertaining to the dried-up and damaged old(er) woman, have not disappeared. Here are a num-

ber of the entries: "breasts atrophy," "breasts shrink," "vagina shrivels," "atrophic mucosal surfaces," "tissues dry out," "atrophic vaginitis," "castration," "clitoral hypertrophy," "damaged body," "dowager's hump," "entire genital system dries up," "eunuch," "femininity abridged," "genital atrophy," "her body betrays her," "sexual neuters," "shrunken hag."

39. The artist wishes to maintain anonymity.
40. Interview with the author, 18 June 1992.
41. The artist wishes to maintain anonymity.
42. Carolee Schneemann quoted in Lucy R. Lippard, *From the Center: Feminist Essays on Women's Art* (New York: Dutton, 1976), 126.
43. Schneemann used "strange origami" in a telephone conversation with the author, 26 June 1993.
44. The artist wishes to maintain anonymity.
45. Jessica Benjamin, "A Desire of One's Own: Psychoanalytic Feminism and Intersubjective Space," in Teresa de Lauretis, ed., *Feminist Studies/Critical Studies* (Bloomington: Indiana University Press, 1986), 78–101, develops many ideas applicable to Schneemann's art.
46. David Joselit makes this mistake in "Projected Identities," *Art in America* 79 (November 1991): 121. He writes, "In its dependence on supposedly timeless symbols of the female body—the violin, fertility figures, the vagina itself—Schneemann's work seems to assert that femininity is something timeless and unchanging and based on the body alone." If Joselit wants an essentialist statement he should read Madonna, *Sex*, ed. Glenn O'Brien (New York: Warner, 1992), unpaginated: "I love my pussy; it is the complete summation of my life. It's the place where the most painful things have happened. But it has given me indescribable pleasure. My pussy is the temple of learning." Joselit should also take note that a vulva is not a vagina.
47. Carter, *The Sadeian Woman*, 128. She wonders, "Could not the object of genital hatred [the mother's vulva] become the object of genital love?" (132).
48. Linda Williams, *Hard Core: Power, Pleasure, and the "Frenzy of the Visible"* (Berkeley: University of California Press, 1989), 34–36, 48–51, 53, 55.
49. Barbara Hepworth quoted in Cassandra Langer, "Against the Grain: A Working Gynergenic Art Criticism," in Raven, Langer, and Frueh, eds., *Feminist Art Criticism*, 125.

HAS THE BODY LOST ITS MIND?

[Frueh steps from a table of panelists to a podium. As she stands up, she takes off her white tailored jacket to reveal a spare peach-pink camisole. The audience gasps, and Frueh is amazed at how small a gesture can be disruptive in an academic setting. Her linen miniskirt is a similar pink, but has a lavender cast. Her stockings are white, her shoes deep rose.]

I called my mother. I was writing a novel and wanted to confirm the details of an incident at the beginning, an accident of blood, based on her experience. She said I had conflated elements from three events, a doctor-induced abortion, a miscarriage, a sudden hemorrhaging when she walked a city sidewalk on a summer day.

[Frueh's voice catches as if she is about to cry.]

She told me more about each happening than I had heard before, and she said too that years later, when maybe she had not needed a hysterectomy, she had been enraged at the doctor. The intensity of memory, current emotion, and understanding brought us close to tears.

[Frueh's voice gains force through volume in the next three paragraphs.]

Maybe I am bleeding now. And maybe you are bleeding too. Maybe all of us are bleeding in more ways than one. Maybe we are hurting for ways to love our bodies, to talk about our blood and hair, our fat and wrinkles, our sexual sensations, our treatment under the hands of lovers and the medical profession, our many changes of life.

Maybe we are searching for erotic ways of living, which express the joy, depth, richness, and responsibility of being human. The erotic is the source and sustenance of wisdom, but Western culture does not understand the erotic—that it can exist in spiritual and political activity and activism, that it can be dead or alive during sex, that it is present in prosaic as well as ecstatic moments. The erotic is expansive, but it has become shrunken due to misunderstandings of it and accommodations to dullness.

Maybe we seek an equilibrium between spiritual and political, a rejection of fear and ignorance of the female body, a state of comfort, which is the lost homeland of the body. For we are not at home in our bodies. We are not sufficiently body-conscious.

Body-consciousness comes from thinking about the body as a base of knowledge and using it as such. Mind is inherent throughout the body.[1] To perceive blood, hair, flesh, senses and their existence in a network of information—social, political, and ecological structures that are the world—is to know that the body is not dumb.

Artists and critics who deal with the voice and intelligence of the female body, especially issues or themes of blood, sex, myth, cunt, womb, breasts, goddesses, and spirituality, are sometimes called essentialist.

Before I define and discuss essentialism, I want you to know that I consider it a misnomer. This is because it is a name given by those who do not engage in what they see as its practice. Essentialism, like Impressionism, is a name given by the opposition. Many feminists, such as Mary Daly, an essentialist *par excellence* if we were to take the term as true, have addressed the significance of naming. On the negative side, those who are named can not only be labeled but, worse, branded and then dismissed through the name.

According to the namers, essentialism is biological determinism, glorification of a female essence, belief that such an essence is transhistorical and transcultural. Essentialists may deal with goddess myths and focus on female deity as idea and presence, as a source of empowerment. Theorists who believe in the term *essentialist* say that because sexuality is socially and culturally constructed, there is no female essence. They say too that female sexuality so constructed is the male-dominant culture's delimiting of women into the bondage of Woman, who is the

Other, marginalized and discounted, not permitted to be a serious shaper of culture. Essentialists, by seeing Woman as Other—sexual, natural, spiritual—maintain women's Otherness and continue women's absence from the cultural dialog.

Artist Judith Barry and film critic Sandy Flitterman-Lewis critique women's art that

> can be seen as the glorification of an essential female power. . . . This is an essentialist position because it is based on the belief in a female essence residing somewhere in the body of woman. . . . Feminist essentialism in art simply reverses the terms of dominance and subordination. Instead of the male supremacy of patriarchal culture, the female (the essential female) is elevated to primary status.[2]

Essentialism is seen as simplistic, a monolithic treatment of the female body, a restereotyping. Appropriation and deconstruction, which are anti-essentialist positions, reject the idea of innate femaleness and the authenticity of women's experiences, which, because they are culturally and socially constructed, cannot be trusted. Essentialism is an artistic affirmation of what film critic Jane Weinstock, writing about Nancy Spero's handmade paper scrolls of women heroes, calls "an Other-worldliness which reinscribes the traditional male/female opposition."[3]

Mary Daly writes about metapatriarchal journeying, away from patriarchy's necrophilic lusts and into a biophilic participation in the reality that human beings are as much earth-substance as are trees, winds, oceans, and animals. Daly's belief that this journeying is "Astral/Archaic" would probably be seen by Weinstock as extremely Other-worldly rather than as bio-logically substantial.[4] (*Bio* means life.)

Certainly sexuality is socially constructed, but it is also bio-logically determined, grounded in the facts that there is a logic to life and that if we avoid this logic, which includes love and knowledge of our bodies, we will suffer in them.

Spero responded to Weinstock's comments. Spero says Weinstock "tries to gag me by her legislating" against myth and the body. Weinstock replies that she intended "to articulate a perspective which would bypass the biological."[5] To bypass the bio-logical is to condemn the female body to absenteeism, not to allow it to speak through the language of its owner. Granted, we all speak through the damage of male dominance, but this does not mean that we must mute the female body until a new vocabulary has been created. For we create the change, and not through bio-logical rejection. We alter reality by asserting our presence, as body, soul, and mind. We combat absence with presence.

Weinstock says that "the Body, . . . exalted by a number of feminist artists, ha[s] become [a] victim of the capital letter."[6] This may be true, but the female body, proscribed by the namers, has also become the victim of fear that anatomy, based on past, patriarchal experience, is an ugly destiny because women's genitals, which, read by patriarchy and by many individual men, appear to provide entry into women's bodies, seem to be the source of women's passiveness, receptivity, and vulnerability. So cunt is the source of inferior human status, and, in essence, a woman is a cunt.

Anti-essentialists believe that artists who represent the female body and critics who applaud this art and deal with the female body as source and site of experience are retrograde. Eleanor Heartney writes in reference to feminism and the '80s, "Suddenly nothing seems more passé than . . . vaginal imagery, body art . . . and all the other forms pioneered by women in response to their particular experience."[7] In the so-called postfeminist '80s, it is fine, even lucrative, to deconstruct man-made images, cultural and media representations of women. But it is retrograde to be a woman who, like Spero or Hannah Wilke, uses the female body as a vehicle for exploring the lost homeland, what has been territory uncharted by women through their own images.

Spero and Wilke, among others, are interested in universalizing the female body as form and metaphor, not through a simplistic reversal of male-as-universal, but, rather, as a declaration of reality: women are present and can create their own meanings. Such work asserts that the body is not simply nature, and these artists do not assume that nature as our culture understands it is natural. In Spero's and Wilke's work, the female body speaks as culture, for its representation realizes the interconnections of art, idea, meaning, history, and bio-logic.

Anti-essentialists seem to think that the body is mind-less, but the body is intelligent and articulate. The body and the unconscious are one, unconscious and tacit knowing are closely related, and body knowledge is a part of all cognition. The opposition, armed with theory from the current voices of authority, who are mostly French and male, armor themselves against the body. They treat the body as ideology and cultural artifact, not as lived-in reality. Anti-essentialism is a technique for management of anatomy as reality.

Reality can be seen as culturally constructed, but it can also be seen as what inescapably is. Experience, accruing different meanings in different eras and cultures, cannot be negated. Yet, like it or not, women menstruate, swell in pregnancy, give birth, go through menopause. Women artists and critics who represent and write (about and from) the body are engaged in a reconstruction of reality, so that the body, loosened from the constraint of an absolutist cultural determination, can speak as an origin of experience, knowledge, and possibility.

The female body can speak from a standpoint of unworkable cliché and self-exploitation, but it can also speak with a terrifying and truthful presence that is anything but Other. Otherness may be the divorce of mind from body, Logos from Eros, escape into the Otherworld of hyperintellectualism.

Feminism is suffering in the '80s from this Otherworldliness, a critical and artistic retreat from the body into a theoretical stratosphere from which the artist or critic observes or analyzes but is not the body. Art is an intellectual endeavor, as is criticism, but the foregrounding of theory incarcerates the mind, so that it is out of touch with the body, isolating the brain from the body. In actuality brain and body are mutually necessary: they are alert to and in love with one another. Body is all mind and mind is all body, they permeate one another, and together they originate information that can initiate erotic wisdom.

After the heat of early '70s feminism, with its angers, militancy, and cunt art, its lack of theory—a retrospective and hyperintellectualist assessment—and its academic unacceptability, we have seen in the past decade, especially in the "postfeminist" '80s, the appropriation of existing images of women for a cool art, disembarrassed of particular experience, disembodied, and we have witnessed the phenomenon of feminism grown frigid through the legitimation of gender studies as practiced by feminists and nonfeminists alike. We have seen feminists proving they are intellectuals. Perhaps this has been necessary, to know, I hope for ourselves, that we are neither simply bodies nor simple bodies. To some degree, however, I see this intellectual production, so much of it ultrasubtle in the employment and elaboration of semiotic, psychoanalytic, and deconstructionist theories, its embracing of Franco-male fashions, as forced labor. Alice Neel said, "Women in this culture often become male chauvinists, thinking that if they combine with men, they may be pardoned for being a hole rather than a club."[8] Fear of the female body separates Logos from Eros. Cunt, and all its derisive connotations, scares us. Cunt is dangerous to professional well-being.

Theory is important. But it need not be written in a dry prose filled with jargon. And scholarship is not by definition compliance with intellectual trends. Theory, stylish and elegant, can become an adornment, a luxurious covering (up) of the body.

Apparently the female body is too bald an issue, but we must find ways to be naked, to uncover whatever it is that we may be.

Hyperintellectual criticism is very much unlike the new art writing, both polemical and poetic, that art historian and critic Moira Roth saw emerging in the '70s.[9] The importance of developing such a language, one rooted in an erotics of the intellect, seems to have fallen by the wayside on the tough road to the lost homeland. If we only *think*—narrowly defined—about the body, our prose will be dispassionate, will close into an academic mold instead of opening into the lushness that grows from mental sensuality and experiential lust.

Knowledge, we believe, is gained through distance from the body. A choice has been made for us: we think with a narrowly defined mind and come up with austere, dis-embodied solutions to problems of living. We (try to) stand outside ourselves, so to merge mind and body consciously, to be erotic about ourselves, is misunderstood as a kind of idolatry, as if women who love the female body in their art and writing will now and forever practice the woman worship that men have promulgated.

Learning and knowing are process, the flow of information—which is emotional, intellectual, and sensuous—throughout a world of political and social structures, of rivers, woods, and deserts, and of human relationships, all of which are alive, which means nonstatic. Women who represent and write (about and from) the body may only be inching away from centuries of outworn myths about women, but measurement is not the point. Movement is.

To participate in the process of living, to be alive, we must act, and we cannot act without our bodies. If we are to take action on our own behalf, to be activists, we need an erotics of the intellect to give ideas body. The wordplay enjoyed by Weinstock in the exhibition review that cites Spero as Other-worldly is erotic to a degree. For example, it is pleasurable to hear and think about Weinstock's question, "Could there be a better way to punish the pundits than with a pun?"[10] Linguistic play and French theories are seductive, but they often serve as stimulations for a certain kind of autoeroticism, which is pleasure on the part of the thinker and initiated readers. Now, autoeroticism is important, for it affirms the subject's knowledge of herself. An erotics of the intellect originates in autoeroticism. However, autoeroticism is insular if its practice does not include outreach, action, interaction, intercourse. Autoeroticism becomes dystopian, as Spero calls Weinstock's view.[11] Autoerotic dystopia is a difficult and ineffective place, a depressing refuge for the homeless, unless the practitioner is moved to speak, write, and act beyond the world of theory.

A better way to punish a pundit than with a pun is to kick her ass, to make her know she has a body and that sensation is real. Disrupting a pundit's linguistic security is good, for language constructs reality, but the body, constructed of blood, bone, hair, flesh, and water, *is* reality.

Essentialists are accused of being unreal, of being actresses playing man-made roles, posing as goddesses, acting as if they are in touch with nature unadulterated by ideology. Women who represent the female body, however, can be activators, of sexual and spiritual potential. They are activists who know that to speak with the body, for themselves, is to speak politically.

At its best, body politics is an erotic practice. So the issue of the female body in art and criticism is not necessarily one of female essence but, rather, one of epistemology, action, and love. Love is distant in theoretical autoerotics because love is action, aliveness in the soul-and-mind-inseparable-from-the-body. The kiss of love is a mouth away. Theory does not kiss us, and we as daughters, mothers, sisters, and even lovers have hardly learned to kiss each other.

My mother kissed me, with her words and heart, when she told me about her accidents of blood, and she said of women, "We're an immense club." I said, "Yes, but we need to know more about each other, to talk about our bodies."

We need to speak about and with our bodies, to make art and writing that kiss us, to know our own wiseblood.

Notes

"Has the Body Lost Its Mind?" is a revision of a paper delivered on the "Theory" panel at "The Way We Look, The Way We See: Art Criticism for Women in the '90s," a conference organized by the Woman's Building in Los Angeles, in January 1988.

A version of this chapter originally appeared in High Performance *12 (Summer* 1989*). That material is reprinted by permission of* High Performance.

1. Morris Berman's *The Reenchantment of the World* (Ithaca: Cornell University Press, 1981) was helpful as I thought about minding the body.
2. Judith Barry and Sandy Flitterman-Lewis, "Textual Strategies: The Politics of Art-Making," in Arlene Raven, Cassandra Langer, and Joanna Frueh, eds., *Feminist Art Criticism: An Anthology* (New York: HarperCollins, 1991), 89. Originally published in *Screen* (Summer 1980).
3. Jane Weinstock, "A Lass, a Laugh, and a Lad," *Art in America* 71 (Summer 1983): 7.
4. Mary Daly, *Pure Lust: Elemental Feminist Philosophy* (Boston: Beacon Press, 1984), 11–12, writes, "The expanse of our Journey is Astral/Archaic and the Voyagers are Archelogians whose Lust is fueled by the influence of the stars."
5. Nancy Spero, "Letters: On Women and Laughter," and Jane Weinstock's reply, *Art in America* 71 (November 1983): 7.
6. Weinstock, "A Lass, a Laugh, and a Lad," 7.
7. Eleanor Heartney, "How Wide Is the Gender Gap?" *Artnews* 86 (Summer 1987): 140.
8. Alice Neel, quoted in Cindy Nemser, "Forum: Women in Art," *Art Talk: Conversations with 12 Women Artists* (New York: Charles Scribner's Sons, 1971), 10.
9. Moira Roth, "Visions and Re-Visions: Rosa Luxemburg and the Artist's Mother," in Raven, Langer, and Frueh, eds., *Feminist Art Criticism*, 99–110. Originally published in *Artforum* (November 1980).
10. Weinstock, "A Lass, a Laugh, and a Lad," 10.
11. Spero, "Letters," 7.

DUEL/DUET

Written and Performed by Joanna Frueh and Christine Tamblyn

[*Frueh and Tamblyn, who, respectively, have sometimes been identified in the art world as a believer in body consciousness and lived experience and as a believer in the social construction of identity, stage a mock debate. The podiums at which they stand form a forty-five-degree angle. Tamblyn wears austere black garments, Frueh a red, leopard-print unitard. Using two slide projectors, first one, then the other speaker shows an image of a female archetype or stereotype and reads a text written by the speaker herself. Each image-and-text combination is a response to the previous combination chosen/produced by the other performer.*

Tamblyn often speaks wryly and once or twice caresses her torso. Frueh's tone is sincere, and she never touches herself. Whether speaking or listening, each performer often looks at her partner.]

CHRISTINE

Image: Goddess images from Lucy Lippard's Overlay, *page 40*

I've always had problems with the goddess as an icon for woman. She seems uncomfortably close to Mr. God—Mr. God in drag, perhaps. During my Catholic childhood, I endured more than enough of Mr.

God with His prohibitions and punishments. I know she is supposed to be different, loving and nurturing. Nevertheless, she still must signify authority; by nurturing or not, she has power over life and death, and to give birth is also to bestow mortality.

But it isn't just the goddess's associations with maternal authority that trouble me. It's also the atavistic nostalgia that contextualizes her—her role in crystallizing the desire to regress to a prepatriarchal, precapitalistic state of wholeness. Our visions of this era are surely mythical, suffused with ideological presumptions that are more valid as projections of repressed aspects of the present than as representations of past milieus. In any case, the truth value of the pseudo-anthropological narrative of the patriarchal usurpation of an original matriarchal culture is not particularly relevant.

What does matter is that the myth itself has no resonance for me. I want to find out what will happen next, not to get stuck in a repetitive groove of the always already known. It's not that I subscribe to Western culture's delusions about progress. I don't presume that everything is improving or that we should proceed along our current course. But neither would I assert that the solution is to revert to past values, even if this were possible. Innocence is not the highest state of consciousness, and flashbacks always resolve into the narrative frame. Perhaps we can devise a time machine so that those who feel more at home in the past may visit it occasionally. I would like to fashion models that bridge dichotomies the way a time machine can, encompassing both the past and the future rather than mandating a choice between them.

JOANNA

Image: Dante Gabriel Rossetti's Astarte Syriaca, *1877*

You begin with an entrapment. Acknowledging this, I don't mind being caught, for I have no captor. An idea, myth, and archetype captivate me, and deep attraction can be a catalyst for change, in this case, the bridging of perhaps fictional pasts and radical futures.

A former student recently asked me what archetypes engage me. I said, "Certain goddesses," paused, and added, "Love and sex goddesses." Like you, the truth value of the pseudo-anthropological narrative doesn't seem relevant to me, but I find the potency of a she-deity provocative.

I titled my dissertation "The Rossetti Woman." From my childhood, when, seeing a couple of Rossetti pieces in a book my parents had I drew the women in them, up through my twenties, his images of women fascinated me. The dissertation was a way for me to explore the goddess image intellectually.

I identified with the Rossetti Woman, who, as his work developed, came to have large, sensuous features and luxuriant hair. Astarte Syriaca: goddess of love and sex, she is a monster here, disproportionate and anything but innocent. I'd always felt that she'd seen it all, been bruised and haunted by love and sex, as had Rossetti. I see her as an erotic icon. I'd like her stance and gaze to be confrontational. She is dreamy, not a dreamer. However, through her I have been an active dreamer, perhaps a monster.

Some find a woman monstrous—shockingly improper or absurd—when she clearly loves her intellect and her sexuality. They may call her self-indulgent and self-absorbed, as though narcissism were negative by definition. Ironically, the projection of self-love generates hate. But we all must dare to be monstrous, to be deviants from the "naturalness" of self-hate and self-erasure.

Astarte's fingers at breast and crotch touch me—the sexual gesture is for me, as well as for male eyes. She is a power, of flesh and thoughtfulness and, paradoxically but necessarily, vulnerability. (Maybe she *does* dream.) She is a romantic lie, what Rossetti in his sonnet "Astarte Syriaca" mystifies as "betwixt the sun and moon a mystery."[1]

Yet in that position she is the unknown, and I can read the unknown as potentiality. I like the idea of female authority, not to the exclusion of male and not as some kind of universal absolute, but as an unknown quantity that can change the construction of erotic postures, both mental and physical.

For all the mothers daughters sons and fathers say
Jesus Christ and God
We call the deities
In hours of unspeakable grace
No one asks for a woman
Venus with her many names
Yours and mine included.

CHRISTINE

Image: Mother's Day Card

The Rossetti woman enthralls me, too, but I am suspicious of her. It would be easy to let her beguile me into a reverie of midnight raptures, but the problem for me is that this is still *his* image of her. What is she thinking? We can only conjecture, since she is mute, her rosebud lips pursed provocatively. You observe that her fingers at her breast and crotch are there for you as well as for him. But who marked those erogenous zones on her body?

Feminist semiotician Kaja Silverman has characterized the female body as already written by patriarchal discursive formations: "The female body is charted, zoned and made to bear meaning, a meaning which proceeds entirely from external relationships, but which is always subsequently apprehended both by the female subject and her 'commentators' as an internal condition of essence."[2]

I fear that his romantic inscriptions construct a different identity for her than she suspects. They lead to her servitude as his slave girl, enchained not by wreaths of flowers but by lines of laundry hung out to dry. When I went to the store to select a Mother's Day card for my mother, I found this image. Its blatantly misogynistic humor was reinforced by the message inside, which reads, "You discover the washer is already full! Happy Mother's Day, anyway!" And this card was not atypical; many of the "funny" cards focused on guilty jokes about mothers' unceasing domestic labors.

So the image of the goddess is an entrapment: the male persuades us to see ourselves in her image and likeness, and soon we are barefoot and pregnant in the kitchen, bearing his children and mopping his floors. As you say, the Rossetti woman is a romantic lie, a sweet nothing. But I don't believe that the truth masked by the lie is an unknown potentiality. Rather, it is revealed in this picture of the endlessly beleaguered housewife.

JOANNA

Image: Models in Azzedine Alaïa dresses, 1987

All images are silent. It is the viewer who gives them voice, creating a romance, moral tale, case history, or horror story.

A woman who wears an Azzedine Alaïa dress can tell different stories. One could be a prelude to beleaguered housewife: sex goddess, clothed in masculine thought, wins a man and is lost, as goddess of the hearth. Maybe the Alaïa women are dressed in the beginning picture of that story. But Alaïa's and Jean-Paul Gaultier's fashions can be proclamations of pleasure that redefine the erotic woman.

Of course the female body has been marked by a patriarchal hand and eye. I appreciate feminist theorists' perceptive and sometimes brilliant analyses of Woman as fetishized image, beautiful object meant for the touch through the gaze, and women, then, intellectually and emotionally grasped as visibly different and sexuality defined as sexual difference established by the fathers.

This has become dominant feminist thinking in academia and the art press, and there it presents dangers. Feminist analyses and interpretations are meant to change our readings of ideologies and realities and thus to empower women in particular. However, such discussions have become overpowering: the eroticized and sexualized woman is object-victim of the male gaze. Consequently, for a woman to think or act otherwise—to use her body in her art in a "seductive" manner, to get herself up in an arousing way—may cause some feminists to perceive her as reactionary.

Reaction need not be backward-looking or dependent. To react is to be alive. Women need to react, in thought and action, to feminist theories, to use theoretical investigations in order to play—in collaboration or contradiction—with dominant masculinist and feminist ideologies.

Using men's fantasies for ourselves can be useful. At the same time, we risk being used. But for the diseases of socially constructed identity a variety of healing treatments are possible. Surgery—cutting out the parts that seem traumatized, limiting the images, fashions, and fantasies that women can entertain—is unhealthy. Such a measure keeps sexuality in crisis, for removing the bad, the patriarchal markings, maintains a schism between the sexes and between gendered looks and gazes.

Edward Abbey, hardly a feminist, but a fascinating thinker about nature and "the wild," equated appearance with reality, for, according to him, a forty-year-old person must assume responsibility for her face. Individual experience marks human beings. We choose our destinies to some extent, inscribe ourselves. Feminism is about inscribing, de-scribing, and re-scribing the self, choices based on new information.

Feminism tells us that anatomy need not be destiny. Therefore breasts, crotch, hips, and ass do not have to lead women into fucking, motherhood, and domestic labor—heterosexuality as a mess. (As an aside, no one, man or woman, with whom I've lived, except my parents, has been as assiduous about housekeeping as I.) At any rate, a woman in a formfitting dress asserts her anatomy, and not necessarily in the anatomy/destiny equation. That equation assumes female passivity. A woman who chooses, with informed self-consciousness, to call attention to her erogenous zones, to her whole body as erogenous, may be asserting her sexuality in ways that confront and counter *his* image of her.

First, the Alaïa look is at once minimal and maximal, studied. It goes against notions of female sexuality as natural. Second, provocation and submission do not absolutely go hand-in-hand. Third, while society demands that women eroticize themselves, it just as strongly stomps on and stamps out women's sexuality. People may admire a sexually intense woman, part of whose presence derives from a sexy look, but people may also call her whore and narcissist or more subtle terms that originate in fear and jealousy. The public expression of female sexuality remains a threat, especially when a woman who enjoys the tools of fashion knows that as a parodistic stereotype she need not be a cartoon, which I sometimes think Madonna is, but, rather, a saboteur. (Maybe cartoons, humor, are sabotage, too.) She can play, and she can demand her own pleasure.

On that note, if a woman's patriarchally marked erogenous zones give her pleasure, should feminism remove them? Mightn't additions be more fun, and more revolutionary?

CHRISTINE

Image: Marionette Lilith from ZONE 3: Fragments for a History of the Human Body, *Part I, page 413*

The question I keep asking is, Who's pulling the strings? The marionette, Lilith, was made by W. A. Dwiggins, an American who designed books and puppets, among other things. Lilith seems to be grieving or hiding her face in shame, but why? As you have remarked, it is the viewer who animates the image, so the viewer as much as the image-maker jerks the doll into action. Yet the dance steps the doll is capable of performing are a function of her articulated limbs, an aspect of the way she is made.

Like you, I maintain that sensual pleasure is of value, even though our puritanical culture continually subsumes it under the empty imperatives of fame and fortune. Like you, I have taken pleasure in exhibiting my body in performance. My first performances in the mid-seventies featured a persona named Flaming Rose, a fading, inept, decadent, screwball stripper. I was campier than a drag queen, but the ironies were compounded because I was an attractive young woman in my twenties impersonating a blowsy middle-aged one. The masochism in my portrayal dismays me now, but the criticality still seems astute: I was satirizing the mechanisms of seduction by simultaneously employing and sabotaging them in full view of my audience.

I wish I could believe it would be possible merely to turn the tables on men—to assert my sexual desires blatantly and actively, to demand that I receive pleasure along with taking pleasure in bestowing it. But I wonder how much we can shape our destinies by flying in the face of convention. Yesterday I watched *A Winter Tan,* a film based on Maryse Holder's letters from Mexico. An American woman in her fifties, Maryse proclaimed that she was going on vacation from feminism as she embarked on a neocolonial bohemian adventure. Like Malcolm Lowry, Arthur Craven, Arthur Rimbaud, Antonin Artaud, and countless others, she exploited the exoticized otherness of a different country as a preserve for licentiousness and transgression. She danced, drank, took drugs, and fucked the natives indiscriminately, writing about it all the while to secure her redemption via assumption into the pantheon of *poètes maudits.*

But try as she might, she couldn't emulate the tawdry glamor of the macho literary lush. Rather, she looked pathetic, lonely, desperate, vulnerable, and ungracefully aged. Maybe it was just a bad movie, but above all she was implausible. Women still aren't free to live as she intended to live, even in countries where their economic hegemony apes the advantages of patriarchal privilege. And in the end the tenuousness of her position was confirmed when she was murdered, presumably another victim of sexual violence.

Who pulls the strings? It is to the advantage of the manipulators to remain invisible, like the black-robed puppeteer disappearing into the shadows. As I said before, I am wary of my own masochism; I do not wish to opt for a fatalistic viewpoint that preempts the potential for change. I realize that the images you have chosen thus far were predominantly positive, whereas mine have been negative. However, I don't believe that the strings cease to be operated when they are not noticed. For our next round, I'd like to suggest an experiment in role reversal. Can you select an image to react *against* this time? I promise to select one I can affirm.

JOANNA

Image: Unknown artist, Martyrdom of St. Barbara, *1447*

Here we have the typical female Christian martyr. She is a figure in legend, not history. She is a virgin. She refuses to recant her beliefs and often rejects a pagan suitor because she is devoted to her heavenly bridegroom. The suitor's father or the virgin's own father turns her over to the Roman authorities, who torture and execute her. The fathers, familial and patriarchal, pull the strings.

In Barbara's story, her father, at her own request, slashes off her head. Then lightning strikes him.

The strings in this picture are the ropes that bind Barbara, so that a man can slice her breast off. This was one of the common tortures inflicted upon virgins who would not renounce their beliefs.

I think about patriarchy's creation of female martyrs, bottoms in the many sadomasochistic rituals of culture, from wife-beating and rape, to Holder's flagrant, lush yet destructive sexuality, to the self-undermining giggles that signal some women's fear of their own seriousness and agency. I think of Western medicine's mastectomies and of electrodes to the genitals of political prisoners, of agonizing trash—snuff movies—and cult classics—*Blue Velvet*—of women made submissive, ripened for murder. I wonder about the relationship between forced and chosen mutilation. I re-read a poem by Karen Finley:

> And when the last man said his violence—
> I knew I couldn't do anything to them so I'd do something to me—
> I went and took a knife and cut out my hole
> But it just became a bigger hole—[3]

The cutting is resistance and desperation, but must women violate ourselves for our beliefs, in order to preserve virginity in its ancient meaning of independence?

(St. Lucy gouged out her eyes, sent them to her suitor.)

How can we keep soul *and* body intact?

Physical mutilation as image or metaphor is powerful, for it rings with integrity: the subject does not disavow her beliefs. But the martyr is to some degree a failure. She may become a hero in death, and thus an inspiration, but I would like leaders rather than martyrs, women who, through living in conviction and conflict, are whole enough to help others get through the big and little tragedies of living with ever less self-violation.

Otherwise, women are bound, like Barbara as S/M bottom.

Sadomasochists believe that S/M is consensual and that the bottom can say No.

Pain and pleasure vary for any individual depending on psychic state and external conditions. Sometimes when my lover and I are fucking with me on my stomach and him on top, I love my hair yanked back then held taut. Sometimes I like him biting my shoulder hard. I read that prolonged, intense pain can cause spiritual ecstasy through transcendence of the body. But, again, I wonder about keeping soul *and* body intact.

I don't want to legislate the morality of sexual pleasures, demand recanting. But I do not see S/M, any more than Barbara's submission to torture, as simply role-playing. Psychological forces and a history of women being forced to submit to tortures great and small, to bondage of mind and body, make the superficial gamesmanship of role-playing impossible. S/M enforces the lesson: women say Yes even when they mean No.

Women in bondage is a stereotype. S/M images of black women position them as slaves, and those of Asian women help a would-be master believe in their pliancy and obedience. The martyr and the masochist are compliant and defiant, good girls and bad. They act on their beliefs, which go against patriarchal authority—don't be a Christian, don't be sexual—yet end up in bondage anyway.

Maryse's story is similar. A woman who loves sex ends up dead because of it. In her book *Give Sorrow Words*, Maryse's voice is one of the most compellingly smart, sensual, graphic, sad, and romantic I've come across.[4] In the book she is crazed, but her frenzy differs from that onscreen because her words move through a reader like a wild and sexy, dirty, luscious fuck. In the film she seems ungracefully aging, not because of her miniskirts and bikinis in tandem with a worn, lined face, but because she lacks grace of presence. In the letters, too, I sense this, that she felt no grace within herself. The actress looks older than Maryse was—thirty-six—when she was killed by her own desire.

Sex slaves become martyrs of love
Our Maryse
Barbara Martyr
    For the love of Christ
    She gave a breast
    donation to the holy order
Barbara means barbarian

Not Amazon
  warring with one bosom
Not Star Bright
  stripping down to sex
  Appealing night after night
Barbara the Barbarian
Just another sideshow
Christ on dead wood still the main attraction
Barbara the Barbarian
Stranger than the fictions of flagellant salvation
Born of barbed wire brains
Bluer than velvet were her eyes
Redder than roseblood
As she prayed
  I wish I may I wish I might
Deader than a doornail
Barbara Ann Barbarian
  Have this wish come true tonight
Holier than thou
You got me rockin' and reelin'
Rockin' with the feelin'
Barbara Ann Barb Barb Barbarian
  May wild fire Father
  Lightning strike
  Your barbed wire brain[5]

CHRISTINE

Image: Pornographic photograph from Caught Looking, *page 13*

My sense of complementarity suggested that I ought to find an image of a man giving pleasure to a woman to respond to your image of men torturing a woman. I did promise to provide a positive image this time.

I decided that the best place to look for such an image would be in *Caught Looking*, a book of pornographic photographs recontextualized for women by the F.A.C.T. Collective. The F.A.C.T. Collective is a feminist group that was formed to combat censorship, particularly the censorship mandated by other feminist factions. *Caught Looking* is a book of commercial photographic pictures selected by the collective from all periods of photographic history. Most of them were not shot by women, since women have never participated in the production of pornography (except as models) until very recently.

In the introduction to *Caught Looking* the authors articulate their intentions:

> In putting out this booklet, we are expressing our belief that the feminist movement must not be drawn, in the name of protecting women, into the practice of censoring 'deviant' sexual representation or expression. . . . Part of becoming sexual subjects involves distinguishing between images of bizarre, forbidden, or even degrading actions, which we may conjure up to excite ourselves sexually from reading, pictures, or memory, and non-fantasized or coerced situations (such as actual rape) over which we have no control.[6]

It seemed appropriate to select a photograph of a man performing cunnilingus on a woman, since this is an activity from which the woman would derive direct clitoral stimulation (no vaginal orgasms here), whereas the man would not be receiving any genital pleasure except through the indirect mode of his own fantasies. I was immediately drawn to this photograph because of the bemused look on the woman's face. What it took me awhile to notice was that the man's index finger was inserted into the woman's anus. At first I was unwilling to acknowledge my fascination with this tabooed erogenous zone. But then I decided that it signified solidarity with male homosexual practices, as well as being a celebration of sexuality divorced from the patriarchal imperatives of procreation and perpetuation of the Name of the Father. It also seemed appropriate that it was his finger, rather than his penis, in her anus, because—as I noted in regard to the oral/genital contact—he was concentrating on her pleasure rather than his own.

The problem I have with positive images is that they tend to be projective; they construct the ideal as an Other, logically positing our own deficiency in comparison. They work in the same way that advertising does, presenting its avatars of wholeness who fill us with anxiety about our own lack, an anxiety that must be assuaged by purchasing a compensatory fetish object. It interests me that you chose a picture that signifies castration anxiety when I requested a negative image. Pardon me if my psychoanalytical interpretation seems too heavy-handed, but the image of a bloody breast being sliced off is so close to castration that any other explanation seems untenable. Not that I would discount my own motive in counteracting the anxiety your picture generates in me by symbolically plugging not one but two holes with a tongue and a finger.

I don't think I can summon the requisite lyricism to write a poem (although I did mentally review the words of the "Hickory Dickory Dock, the mouse ran up the clock" nursery rhyme). I also feel compelled to reply to your description of the "self-undermining giggles that signal some women's fear of their own seriousness and agency." My interpretation of the significance of humor is quite different. Hélène Cixous has referred to "the revolutionary power of women's laughter."[7] Comedy may be a successful subversive strategy for those who are still cast in the role of the oppressed and hence weak. I am reminded of Mary Russo's excellent article about the "female grotesque," in which she applied to the female body Mikhail Bakhtin's ideas about carnivals as festivals of temporary role reversal.[8] In your criticism of Karen Finley for internalizing male violence against women, I think you are missing the efficacy of her humor. Her satirical disruptions allow us to look outside the consensual framework of culture, momentarily obstructing business as usual. Of course, these glimpses of freedom may partially defuse tension, thereby helping to reconcile us to our lot. But when comics become daring enough in their violation of taboos, they are inevitably censored for taking us far enough outside social reality for us to be able to strategize about how we might stay there longer.

JOANNA

Image: Women bodybuilders, FLEX (March 1989): 62–63

"Huge and Hard." That's the title of the featured training story in the March 1989 *FLEX,* a bodybuilding magazine that contains these pictures of women who are top heavyweight competitors in the 1988 Women's World Amateur Championships. Competitive bodybuilder Gary Strydom wrote the article, which is about his own training. Yet *huge* and *hard* are words that can describe female as well as male bodybuilders, for in the short history of women's bodybuilding, since the late 1970s, the winners have exhibited ever greater mass and leanness.

I can think of the woman bodybuilder as displaying disruptive excess: she is grotesquely gorgeous. As *FLEX* writer Laura Dayton says, "It was like watching the Biblical waters part when Hannie Van Aken, with her explosion of blond hair and that mind-boggling upper body encased in a bright red mini-top, sauntered through the [hotel] crowd seemingly oblivious to the shockwave she left in her wake."[9] Holland's Van Aken placed second.

The hyperbolic prose describes the effect of a hyperbolic body, which is a joke. The heavyweight especially twists the terms of femininity, power, and strength, and the so-called sculptor of such a body can laugh at the onlooker's shock. The viewer may laugh too, believing that Van Aken and her like are ridiculous. But such a laugh comes from discomfort, for the heavyweights are terrors, phallic women who have displaced the hyperbolically masculine desire to be hard.

Strydom writes, "As for my tendency to get big and stay hard, it's just a genetic thing." ("Genetics" is a cliché in the mythos of bodybuilding.) More Strydom: "You constantly have to think in terms of maintaining both size and hardness." Dayton describes Van Aken as "harder" than her Argentine competitor, who placed fourth.[10]

The heavyweights may be jokers in the deck of femininity, but they may not be wild cards at all, for in their exhibition of size and hardness they may be woman as glorious representation of the phallus, woman literally embodying man's fantasy of himself at his most masculine, the ithyphallic woman. Also, the bodybuilder may say she feels animal, suggesting natural wildness, but she cultivates her physique through diet, training in a gym, and steroids. Drug testing took place at the Women's World, but the owner of my favorite gym, in Tucson, says there's no way to win a major competition without drugs.

I think of another "heavyweight" body, one our society calls overweight. I sat in Savannah, oak trees dripping Spanish moss in the mugginess of deep June. A large woman crossed the square, high heels emphasizing her saunter, which was part of the sensuous confidence she projected. A stylish outfit—black skirt to midcalf and a black blouse with long sleeves—bared little of her dark brown skin. What a contrast this picture is to Laura Creavalle, who won first place in the Women's World and represented her native Guyana while maintaining Canadian citizenship. Creavalle said, regarding strategy for her next and more prestigious competition, "I feel I still need more mass in my quads. And maybe a little more abs," which Dayton describes as already "razor-edged."[11]

I see both Creavalle and the woman in Savannah as intriguing in their departures from Jane Fonda and Cher as feminine standards. Perhaps neither of the first two is healthy: I do not advocate either training or eating to excess, though they fascinate me. For excess implies a normative ideal, and Creavalle and the large woman disrupt that ideal. Their bodies are too much, examples of the immoderate, like the clitoris.

The clitoris is unnecessary for reproduction but essential to pleasure, necessary to biology defined as life- (*bio*) wisdom (*logy*). In conventional terms, the female body that is large is biologically unnecessary, but in life-wisdom, largeness is presentness, a bald statement of living in a body and of pleasure, askew perhaps but active, pleasure in the flesh and pleasuring the flesh.

Combinations of psyche and circumstance design the shape of a body as they do the catalysts of a person's laughter. I concede humor in Finley, but that image, cutting out the hole, remains isolated for me in a vivid, horrifying, and humorless way.

My statement to which you responded has to do with particular women I've known, two who smiled almost constantly and one who giggled during serious conversations in which I and others needed to conduct business. Such expressions and behavior I see as the self-erasure of ingratiation or an unconscious and inordinate desire to please.

Laughter, I agree, is powerful and subversive. A while back, I did say that humor is probably sabotage. Laughter is good for oneself and as a tool with enemies. I hope to use laughter in the future when I run into recently made enemies. I don't want to laugh in their faces, but, rather, greet them with honest good cheer, which I see as derailing nastiness and absorbing the enemy. The technique requires emotional fluidity, not the control that comes from anxiety.

I love the uncontrollable and unpredictable elements of laughter, which can be at once lightweight and heavyweight.

CHRISTINE

Image: Marcel Duchamp's LHOOQ, *1919*

So—phallic women. Is Marcel Duchamp's Mona Lisa with a moustache a phallic woman? Certainly she has hot pants. In a way she is defaced, like the woman the Joker threw acid at in *Batman*, or like Cindy Sherman's recent disfigured self-portraits. Body art, bodybuilding, plastic surgery, and tattooing are all indexical practices that leave their mark on the body. Marcel Duchamp added a signifier of maleness to the image of a woman, thereby producing a contradictory sign. He also symbolically wrecked a canonical masterpiece of Western art, just as the Joker did during his destructive rampage in the art museum. The Mona Lisa as the enigmatic, fascinating epitome of womanliness is demystified by Duchamp's sarcastic gesture. She's removed from her high art pedestal by the irreverence of Duchamp's populist graffito. No longer the artist's muse, she becomes a hermaphroditic monster in Angela Carter's sense: "A free woman in an unfree society will be a monster."[12]

Artistic creativity is narcissistic activity, a separation from the mother that nevertheless maintains formal, symbolic, and libidinal connections to the maternal body. By adding a moustache to the Mona Lisa Duchamp recreates her in his own image and likeness. Mona Lisa fetishized, the fetish object always a substitute for the impossible female phallus. The interdependence of masculine and feminine functions unified in the mythical figure of the androgyne.

The fundamental rhetorical trope of surrealism is Lautréamont's juxtaposition of an umbrella and a sewing machine on a dissecting table. The umbrella phallic and the sewing machine female/domesticized. The dissecting table the theater of operations. Duchamp's art, like Lautréamont's, utilizes readymade objects and radical juxtapositions.

The Mona Lisa recently made the news. Some art historian discovered that her face was Leonardo da Vinci's own, and, furthermore, that he was a homosexual who was rendering his self-portrait in drag. That Gioconda smile! Duchamp had prefigured this shocking disclosure by restoring the evidence of the model's real sex. Somehow he had known all along. Laura Mulvey writes, in "Film, Feminism, and the Avant-Garde," "Thus the image of woman in patriarchal representation refers primarily to connotations within the male unconscious, to its fears and fantasies."[13] Mona Lisa's moustache is overdetermined, a phallic substitute on top of a phallic substitute.

But enough of psychoanalytic theory and avant-garde gestures of negation. Like you, I often get fed up with the totalizing rigor of theory. How dare it presume to explain everything! Ever since I repudiated the Catholicism I was indoctrinated into as a child, I have been suspicious of systematic principles and didactic prescriptions. But my refuge against theory is not body knowledge or body language. Rather, it is an appreciation of the quotidian and the aleatory. The complex exigencies of daily life never cease to astonish me. Experience is an inexhaustible gift—more than we can ever perceive or analyze happens to us. Although I would not deny that experience is always ideologically inflected, a surplus residue of randomness or noise remains. Because feminism is itself a theory, its explanatory power sometimes seems oppressive. As Daniel Schreber asserts in *Memoirs of My Nervous Illness,* perhaps the most pleasant form of liberation is the freedom to think about nothing.[14]

JOANNA

Image: Salvador Dali, The Phenomenon of Ecstasy, *1933*

The freedom to think about nothing is the smile of ecstasy, of knowing something without thinking, though maybe it has been thought through countless ways, thousands of years, by mind upon mind.

The freedom to think about nothing stops when I must ask, Is this, the phenomenon of ecstasy, a fantasy produced within the male unconscious? Is female ecstasy a joke?

The freedom to think about nothing feels like love, and love is not a joke.

Theory can make love a joke—a romantic trap, a betrayal of woman's desire, a ridiculous impossibility. But love remains recognizable, even when it has been twisted by sniggers, theory, and broken hearts. Love can be cruel, can be deconstructed, but it is central—the amazements of everyday intricacies, rockbottom beneath the unpredictable.

[*Joanna projects an image of Christine sitting at her desk. Christine asks questions and Joanna responds.*]

How can women gain access to the status of a fully empowered speaking subject without appropriating the male authoritarian voice?

For two days I've felt nauseous and have had diarrhea. Something must come out. Something needs release. My voice is speaking, in shit, unwanted food—too much fat and sugar, I think, not my usual diet last week. I am speaking, in mind-and-soul-inseparable-from-the-body. I don't think this is the male authoritarian voice.

I speak in bits and dribbles, as I'm thinking about many things—mortality and marriage, making money, demoralizing institutions, isolation, friends who are too far away, having a child. Your question is part of my litany of everyday crises. Christine, all I can offer you now are fragments.

But the mind-and-soul-inseparable-from-the-body is whole.

• • •

How can women discover their own authenticity through representations of themselves when all representations are imbued with falsity and simulation?

The mind-and-soul-inseparable-from-the-body has its poetics, its authenticity, and I am listening as best I can. I have no choice if I want to learn from my own sickness, let go of it, and gain new health.

I look at the picture of you, the representation of a writer, I see you here with me, I could be driven crazy by your questions, you are a muse to me.

I think of a picture of me, as the lover, and I would love to come up with answers we could all put in practice as soon as they were spoken. But I am not The Word. And thus I disobey it. Everyone does, to some degree. Yet they fear their disobedience or cannot even acknowledge it.

I must disobey the imperative, implicit in your language, to answer your questions in as intellectual a way as they are asked. For I desire our engagement in ways that argued answers will not satisfy. This desire is success, for you and I together, mind-and-soul-inseparable-from-the-body, are answers.

Our being here, both of us posing as sex and intellect, feminist and skeptic, observer and observed, could be negatively dangerous, keeping energy within the same old two-term circuit. But being both terms breaks the circuit, for if one can be two, then one can be multiple, can take many positions, embody many possibilities.

This does make me want to puke. I fear the possibilities are simply fragments without integrity. I'm afraid that in being many, I am none.

How can women avoid being reduced to or conflated with their bodies, mere procreative wombs and nurturing breasts, desiring-machines to perpetuate the name of the father?

For comfort, with your question and with my love and terror of living in, with, and because of my body, I remember times of acute learning, which are times of integrity. During one, I was rock-climbing, failing after several attempts at a move my partner was coaching me to do. "Squeeze the rock and stand on your left leg. Use your strength," he said. It's hard to explain how terrifying standing up can be, how strange an embrace with rock can feel—a pushing and pulling that moves the climber into deeper intimacy with it—how pleasurable is the success that comes from balance, power, commitment, and grace, from listening to the mind-and-soul-inseparable-from-the-body.

I squeezed, stood, and reached with the poetics of the mind-and-soul-inseparable-from-the-body. Obeying that beauty is disobedience, for the mind and soul and body separated are subject to The Word, The Naming, the simulations and representations we know too well to know them at all. Mind-and-soul-inseparable-from-the-body is integrity, as is love—balance, power, commitment, and grace—which can hold together the seeming fragments of a body politic.

How can we as feminists fashion a movement that does not reduplicate the power structure and strictures of male hierarchies with their emphasis on correct behavior and rigid adherence to the party line?

Love is disobedience in a hate-filled world.

Love is the answer to your questions.

[*Christine projects an image of Joanna kissing her lover open-mouthed. Joanna asks questions and Christine responds.*]

What is a kiss?

A kiss is the sign of a contract, as in the phrase "sealed with a kiss." A more intimate form than a handshake, it signifies women as property to be exchanged, possessions to be owned. At the culmination of the wedding ceremony, the kiss ratifies the marriage contract, according to which, by the Law of the Father, a woman promises to "love, honor, and obey" her husband, servicing only his sexual needs and bearing only his children.

Am I a woman?

According to Freud, the hysteric asks, "Am I a woman?" Unable to speak, the hysteric produces symptoms instead. Her body remembers and expresses the pain she has repressed and cannot name. It is through pain, the pain of separation from the mother, that we each come to know ourselves, assuming male or female identities. Never firmly fixed, these identities are hypothetical and therefore shifting and unstable.

Is this the tongue of love? What are its theory and practice?

The tongue of love may be a euphemism for the phallus as signifier or linguistic marker. Its theory and practice entail division and conquest.

The theory is the division into opposites, with male/female serving as the pattern for the parallel divisions of culture/nature and mind/body. Once the division is made in theory, the conquest occurs in practice, so that one term is privileged over the other: male over female, culture over nature, and mind over body.

How does one become a practiced lover, practiced in love?

We cannot practice love (synthesis) without analysis, because love is not all we need to cross the great divide. As women, we can love ourselves, each other, and men, but we must also learn to give voice to our oppression as part of the struggle against it. Both love and struggle involve negotiation; our lives are comprised of duels and duets. We can affirm our differences, not in the spirit of liberal tolerance or uncommitted relativism, but in acknowledgment of the provisionality of resolution.

Notes

"Duel/Duet" has been performed at:
NAME *Gallery, Chicago, Illinois, November 1989*
Women's Caucus for Art Conference, New York, New York, February 1990
Southern Exposure Gallery, San Francisco, California, December 1990
Yolanda Lopez performed with Christine Tamblyn and myself at Southern Exposure.

1. Dante Gabriel Rossetti, "Astarte Syriaca," in Jerome H. Buckley, ed., *The Pre-Raphaelites* (New York: Modern Library, 1968), 153.
2. Kaja Silverman, "Histoire d'O: The Construction of a Female Subject," in Carol S. Vance, ed., *Pleasure and Danger: Exploring Female Sexuality* (London: Routledge and Kegan Paul, 1985), 325.
3. Karen Finley, "Why Can't This Veal Calf Walk?" *Whole Earth Review* (Summer 1989): 49.
4. Maryse Holder, *Give Sorrow Words: Maryse Holder's Letters from Mexico* (New York: Grove Press, 1979).
5. I play with Bobby Vinton, "Blue Velvet," Epic 9614, and the Beach Boys, "Barbara Ann," *Party!* Capitol DMAS-2398.
6. Kate Ellis, Barbara O'Dair, and Abby Tallmer, "Introduction" to F.A.C.T. Collective, ed., *Caught Looking: Feminism, Pornography and Censorship* (New York: Caught Looking, 1986), 6.
7. Hélène Cixous, "The Laugh of the Medusa," trans. Keith Cohen and Paula Cohen, *Signs* 1, no. 4 (1976): 45.

8. Mary Russo, "Female Grotesques: Carnival and Theory," in Teresa de Lauretis, ed., *Feminist Studies/Critical Studies* (Bloomington: Indiana University Press, 1986).
9. Laura Dayton, "Caribbean Conflict," *FLEX* (March 1989): 64.
10. Gary Strydom, "Huge and Hard," *FLEX* (March 1989): 25, 27, and Dayton, "Caribbean Conflict," 66.
11. Dayton, "Caribbean Conflict," 106.
12. Angela Carter, *The Sadeian Woman and the Ideology of Pornography* (New York: Pantheon, 1978), 27.
13. Laura Mulvey, "Film, Feminism, and the Avant-Garde," *Visual and Other Pleasures* (Bloomington: Indiana University Press, 1989), 122.
14. Daniel Schreber, *Mémoires d'un neuropath* (Paris: Seuil, 1975), 67.

HANNAH WILKE

The Assertion of Erotic Will

The divinity Venus occupied Hannah Wilke for twenty-five years. She pictured herself as a contemporary goddess of love, sex, and beauty, and she also presented herself as a worshipper. Wilke's continual remodeling of Venus from a sex object into a healer of social ills and of Wilke's cancer, from which she died on 28 January 1993 at the age of fifty-two, is an assertion of erotic will.

Wilke's *Venus Envy* (1980) recalls Gustave Courbet's *Woman with a Parrot* (1863). In both works a female nude with luxuriant tousled hair lies on the floor voluptuously displaying her beautiful body. Courbet's woman exemplifies the phenomenon in Western art of male artists creating The Beauty with whom they become identified, an individualized Venus. Other obvious examples include the women painted by Boucher, Titian, Rossetti, Renoir, and Modigliani. The Beauty has verified male "genius," and art history names men as geniuses of feminine beauty, inventors through the centuries of a variety of types who, in their own time and perhaps later, can be perceived as models of female attractiveness and desirability.

Although women such as Marie-Louise Elizabeth Vigée-Le Brun, Marie Laurencin, Romaine Brooks, Frida Kahlo, and Léonor Fini have represented female beauty, their work in this area has not often been given equal status with even second-rank depictions by men. In this light, a woman's choice to deal directly with female beauty in her art does seem inspired, both as a blunt recognition of the significance of female beauty in Western art and as an indication of willingness to risk proclaiming the pleasures of beauty for the self. That is an erotic choice. The risk entails excoriation, for society still wants a woman to perform its desires and excitements, not her own. Granted, to isolate a woman's pleasures from society's is impossible, but we must be careful not to attack a woman's declaration of self-pleasure as simply an expression of a negatively feminine narcissism. No woman is that easily categorizable.

Wilke deals with Venus as a metaphor for the beautiful woman. Titles of several of her works—*Venus Envy, Venus Basin, Venus Cushion,* and *Venus Pareve* among them—indicate concern with ideal beauty, and this involvement extends into Wilke's use of herself as the model woman. The nude works she made in her thirties exhibit Wilke's body to advantage. She is whole-limbed and white-skinned, slender and well-proportioned—her breasts are neither "too" large nor "too" small, and her hips are not "too" wide. Her abundant dark hair echoes the traditional symbolism in which lush hair signifies sexual power and dark hair indicates a femme fatale. Wilke enhances her delicately attractive facial features with makeup but never overdoes it. Unshaved armpit hair emphasizes the sexy reality of her.

Wilke's beauty provides her entry into an ideal whose oppressiveness for women threatens to make her work a continuation of the "tyranny of Venus," which Susan Brownmiller says a woman feels whenever she criticizes her appearance for not conforming to prevailing erotic standards.[1] However, Wilke as usual twists language, in this case the grammar of Venus, the perfect woman. She parses the "sentence" of the female body into a statement of pleasure as well as pain. While "modeling" her beauty in *S.O.S.—Starification Object Series* (1974–1975), she "scars" herself with chewing-gum sculptures, suggesting that being beautiful is not all ease, fun, or glamor. Twisting chewed gum in one gesture into a shape that reads as vulva, womb, and tiny wounds, she marks her face, back, chest, breasts, and fingernails with the gum-shapes before she assumes high-fashion poses. Her "scarification" is symbolically related to African women's admired keloided designs on their bodies. The Africans endure hundreds of cuts without anesthesia, and Wilke alludes to the suffering that Western women undergo in rituals of beautification.

From Una Stannard in 1971 to Naomi Wolf in 1991, feminists have analyzed the pain women "choose" in order to meet beauty standards.[2] The beautiful woman suffers, for to be a star as a woman is to bear "starification," being observed by others as a process of criticism and misunderstanding. To be "starified" is, in some measure, to be ill-starred, and the "ornaments" decorating Wilke in *S.O.S.* are not only scars but also stigmata. They make the model woman into a martyr.

Western culture fearfully reveres Venus in the bodies of women, and she must be crucified. Freudian theory kills the mother, not the father, despite the privileged status of the oedipal stage; artist Carolee Schneemann says Dionysus stole ecstasy from Aphrodite; and Wilke believes that Venus envy, not penis envy, has caused misery between women and men. If Venus were a contemporary divine ideal for women, rather than a clichéd sex goddess, then women would not have to struggle to invent the meaning and practice of erotic-for-women.[3]

Erotic-for-women—*for* women meaning that women are producers and consumers—is erotic for oneself, autoerotic autonomy whose power is both self-pleasuring and relational. Autoeroticism is apparent in self-exhibition and in women's gaze at other women unclothed. Erotic-for-women loves the female body without discriminating against its old(er) manifestations. Self-exhibition may demonstrate the positive narcissism—self-love—that masculinist eros has all but erased, and self-exhibition is a commanding statement, "Here I am. See my body," an attitude apparent throughout Wilke's work.

The beautiful resemble other groups that are feared, envied, and hated for their marks of difference. As Wilke says, "Starification-scarification/Jew, black, Christian, Moslem. . . . Labeling people instead of listening to them. . . . Judging according to primitive prejudices. 'Marks-ism' and art. Fascistic feelings, internal wounds, made from external situations."[4]

Wilke remembers that as a girl she "was made to feel like shit for looking at myself in the mirror" and that as a young woman she felt she "was observed, objectified by beauty." Her looks made her uncomfortable, and she believes she is "the victim of my own beauty," for "beauty does make people mistrust you." A woman is "unfeminine," wrong, when she is not beautiful, yet if she is beautiful, she is still wrong. Wilke employs the peculiar inappropriateness of beauty in order to confront its wrongness. By being "improper," publicly displaying her beauty, she has used her art "to create a body-consciousness for myself," a positive assertion of her beauty, which is erotic-for-women.

"Why not be an object?" she asks, one who is aware of her I-ness, who is an "I Object."[5] Wilke's *I Object* (1977–78) critiques Marcel Duchamp's *Etant donnés*, one of his two most mythicized works. *I Object* is a fake book jacket, and its subtitle is *Memoirs of a Sugargiver*. On the front and back Wilke lies nude, legs apart, like the naked girl lying corpselike on twigs in *Etant donnés*. The photographs are what Wilke calls "performalist self-portraits," with artist Richard Hamilton, taken on coastal rocks at Cadaques, Spain, Duchamp's home in Europe during his later years. Two art historians see Duchamp's girl as "locked into a world of her own, like Sleeping Beauty."[6] "I object," as a declaration, protests the girl's inertness. Wilke seems to respond to the girl's deadness when she says, "I find *Etant donnés* repulsive, which is perhaps its message. She has a distorted vagina. The voyeuristic vulgarity justifies impotence."[7]

Etant donnés is a voyeur's dream: viewers can see the naked body only one at a time through a peephole, they look directly at the girl's genitals, and she is eerily passive. Wilke activates her image, reproducing it upside-down on the front cover. On the back cover, the image is right side up. She suggests a turning around of meaning that is a revolt against Duchamp's misshapen, desexed woman. Wilke and Duchamp both love puns and the erotic, and "I object" as a double noun—"eye object" as well as the personal pronoun—acknowledges Wilke's participation as sex object, focus of the voyeuristic gaze, and gives her piece a more explicitly erotic significance than *Etant donnés*. For "I object" is a statement of presence and self-knowledge, and of pride in the delight of receiving a sexually scrutinizing and admiring look and of being able to give pleasure. The subtitle *Memoirs of a Sugargiver* reinforces this interpretation, for Wilke sees herself as a "sugargiver instead of a salt cellar." She offers the sweets of eroticism and beauty. ("Salt cellar" is the anagrammatic play on Marcel Duchamp's name that is the subtitle of Michel Sanouillet's and Elmer Peterson's *The Essential Writings of Marcel Duchamp: Salt Seller = Marchand du Sel.*)

Wilke does not sell out or submit to Duchamp's genius for cool, allusive eroticism. He says that eroticism in his art has been "always disguised, more or less." Not so with Wilke, and, ironically, Duchamp's understanding of the purpose of eroticism in art better describes Wilke's work than it does his. He says that eroticism is "really a way to bring out in the daylight things that are constantly hidden. . . . To be able to reveal them, and to place them at everyone's disposal—I think this is important because it's the basis of everything, and no one talks about it."[8]

The I Object is the object of her own gaze; she knows the body through eyeing as well as aying it, assenting to its beauty. The I Object is her own voyeur and seer, who comes to realize that to seduce is to lead astray, to lure herself and others away from their habitual negations of the erotic. Wilke calls the gaze "a sparkle." The gaze is sparkling eyes, the spark of desire, an "assertion of life," she says, then continues: "To be or not to be. To look or not to look."[9] Erotic looking and sparking are not only sexual desire but also love, life force and instinct, and lust for living.

Feminism has looked at female beauty, but insufficiently. Although the popular success of Naomi Wolf's *The Beauty Myth: How Images of Beauty Are Used Against Women* (1991) demonstrates the magnitude of women's preoccupation and problems with beauty, beauty as an issue has embarrassed feminists and been low on the feminist agenda. In 1983, almost twenty years after the beginning of the second wave and ten years after Wilke created *S.O.S.,* scholars Robin Lakoff and Raquel Scherr admitted that they had talked about beauty "often enough . . . , but informally and personally. We hadn't thought of beauty as a problem or a Problem—not a feminist issue, not at all something you brought up as a serious thought in public." Why? Because Lakoff and Scherr and their serious, feminist, intellectual friends had told themselves that thinking about beauty was vain, self-indulgent and self-absorbed. Lakoff and Scherr discovered, however, that beauty might be "the last great taboo, the anguish that separates women from themselves, men, and each other."[10] Susan Brownmiller earlier came to a similar conclusion in *Femininity,* naming "the struggle to approach the feminine ideal" as "the chief competitive arena . . . in which the American woman is wholeheartedly encouraged to contend."[11] Historian Lois Banner offers a different perspective on the situation in *American Beauty*. "The pursuit of beauty," she says, "has more than any other factor bound together women of different classes, regions, and ethnic groups and constituted a key element in women's separate experience of life."[12] Wilke points to this common cause in *S.O.S.* by presenting photos of herself in playful yet bleakly comic poses and costumes denoting social positions and modes of glamor: a maid's apron, hair curlers, cowboy hat, sunglasses, Arab headdress, Indian caste mark, and, finally, the gum sculptures that resemble African cicatrization wounds.

Because the demand for beauty divides women and yet binds them to each other, Wilke's focus on beauty is a significant public discourse that sees everyday matters as the important concerns they are. When she says that to many people "the traditionally beautiful woman is the stereotype. . . . But nobody says there is a prejudice against beautiful people," she is stating her situation, her own separateness, which is as real for the beautiful woman as for the plain woman.[13]

Wilke's seemingly privileged position has sometimes caused misunderstanding of her art. In 1976 Lucy Lippard wrote that Wilke's "confusion of her roles as beautiful woman and artist, as flirt and feminist, has resulted at times in politically ambiguous manifestations that have exposed her to criticism on a personal as well as on an artistic level."[14] In a misogynist society the beautiful woman enjoys a kind of admiration and respect not given to many women, and such good fortune turns other women against the beautiful woman, snares them in "Venus envy," a phrase first used by Wilke in a 1980 series of Polaroid photographs.

Wilke destabilizes Venus envy, the devaluation of beauty and the erotic practiced by both women and men, by reworking myths and stereotypes about the beautiful woman. People often link beauty and femininity and regard the latter as a set of limitations. Femininity requires artifice, self-control, and perfection in bodily and gestural details, and culture constructs feminine women as needy. The beauty, then, lacks spirit and independence.

Hannah Wilke Can (1974–78) scrambles the terms of femininity. Each can, slotted to accept coins and decorated with three images of a Christ-like Wilke in a loincloth, is a complex handling of the issue of neediness. The cans are for giving to a charity. They were exhibited at a 1978 performance at the Susan Caldwell Gallery in New York called *Hannah Wilke Can: A Living Sculpture Needs to Make a Living*. The Christ-Venus image on the can is one of twenty photographs of her 1974 performance

Hannah Wilke Super-T-Art. Venus is a Western superstar and supertart, a sugargiver *par excellence*. Christ is an ultimate "pinup"—pinned to a cross with nails—as is Venus, whom I referred to above as a crucifixion victim. Christ was a poor man, needy, yet a bestower of charity, *caritas*, Christian love. Wilke the sugargiver is also a giver of charity, even though she requests money for her Venus-Christ. With self-conscious absurdity she asks for professional support as a woman/artist. The slot/slit is a symbolic cunt, and Wilke-Venus is a sacred whore, for *caritas* actually means grace, specifically the grace of the

> Triple Goddess, embodied in the boon-bestowing Three Graces who dispensed *caritas* (Latin) or *charis* (Greek) and were called the Charities. . . .
>
> Romans sometimes called grace *venia*, the divine correlative of Venus. . . . Grace meant the same as Sanskrit *karuna*, dispensed by the heavenly nymphs and their earthly copies, the sacred harlots of Hindu temples. . . . Their "grace" was a combination of beauty, kindness, mother-love, tenderness, sensual delight, compassion, and care. . . .
>
> Christians took the pagan concept of *charis* and struggled to divest it of sexual meanings. . . . The cognate word *charisma* meant Mother-given grace.[15]

In *Hannah Wilke Can* the beautiful woman, the charismatic, speaks of the need for love and couples it with the self-assertions "I can support myself" and "I can support Venus, love, and beauty."

Wilke counters the "femininity" of control and perfection because she does not use beauty as a trick to cover up emotion. The beauty's face in art and the media is often bland in order to divest her of character or feeling, so that viewers can project their own desire onto the woman. Many of the *So Help Me Hannah* photographs (1978–81), in which Wilke, dressed only in high heels and brandishing a gun, poses in a gritty environment, show her face in strain, as a sign of alertness or fatigue, pain or expectancy. The videotape *Gestures* (1974) most extremely combats the stereotypical beauty's necessary inexpressiveness. Here Wilke manipulates her face with her hands, using her skin as sculptural material. She pinches, pulls, slaps, smooths, and caresses her face, shaping it into grotesque and ridiculous gestures that externalize and exorcise inner crisis.

So Help Me Hannah Series: Portrait of the Artist with Her Mother Selma Butter (1978–81) is a blunt and poignant handling of women's "perfection" and "imperfection." Wilke appears in the diptych's left segment with her breasts and chest displaying found objects that resemble "raygun" shapes she had collected as gifts for her lover, Claes Oldenburg, in the early 1970s. She scrutinizes the viewer wearing an expression that suggests that pain and sadness underlie her flawless complexion. On the right Wilke's mother has turned her face from the camera, and her body, exposed from shoulders to waist, shows not only an old woman's fragility but also the ravages of disease. Selma Butter has had a mastectomy, and the scars of her cancer surgery cover the area where her breast once was.

Wilke's "guns" and her youthfulness and beauty in the photograph allude to cover-girl shots, a phrase that reads as a pun: the beautiful, young, model woman "shot" by a camera, murdered into a still, an ideal picture of femininity, the cover girl who covers up her imperfections with emotional and actual makeup. Wilke's indication of trouble in the paradise of beauty—the guns as emotional scars of lost love—becomes real scarification in the portrait of her mother. Wilke uncovers truth—that life is also loss, that beauty changes, that age and illness must not be hidden. We see a deteriorated body that the photographer, Wilke, clearly loves, for it is very much alive with the presence of Selma Butter. Here perhaps is the necessary correlate of Wilke's erotic joy—the reality of death.

Wilke faced both of these in 1987 when she was diagnosed with cancer—lymphomas in her neck, shoulders, and abdomen—and from then till her death, in the art she made during her illness. The *INTRA-VENUS Series* (1992–93) is an astounding assertion of erotic will, which proves that erotic-for-women is courageous and radical. *INTRA-VENUS* is a rite of passage for illness and aging.

Germaine Greer says in *The Change: Women, Aging and the Menopause* that society provides no rite of passage for menopausal women, and she writes, too, about the pleasures of becoming a matron, which include tending to spiritual well-being and to one's garden and becoming invisible.[16] Many women say that at around fifty they did begin to feel invisible, but that, contrary to Greer's assessment, the experience is frustrating, demeaning, and shocking. (Greer advises that once a woman gets used to invisibility and understands its value, which is the pleasure of being left alone, she will be satisfied.) I read and hear about Croning rituals, in which women name and celebrate their entry into elderhood. Croning makes old(er) women visible—respected and powerful—to themselves, but croning is not every old(er) woman's answer to the changes that aging brings her. Croning seems like a New Age escape to some women, a romantically spiritual exercise.

INTRA-VENUS records Wilke's rite of passage and provides a terrifying enlightenment for the initiate-viewer. Wilke continued her autoerotic self-portrait focus in an attempt to "treat" herself with love during what she called her "beauty to beast" transformation.[17] In an erotophobic society Wilke, along with such other artists as Carolee Schneemann and Joan Semmel, originated a feminist visual erotics, and she continued into her early fifties to liberate women from the male gaze as theoretical orthodoxy and as actual hatred and misunderstanding of women's sensual and visual pleasures. These, Wilke understood, might differ from male-dominant erotic dogma if women explored and released them.

Numerous feminist writings mothered by Laura Mulvey's "Visual Pleasure and Narrative Cinema," first published in 1975, have denied women the authenticity of their own visual and bodily experiences and have imprisoned women in the accepted reductiveness of the male gaze.[18] But the female gaze, in its genuineness and legitimacy and its relation to women's erotic pleasure, is a radical agent of change. The erotic provides the means for reinventing oneself, which Wilke does in *INTRA-VENUS*. She also reinvents the female nude more aggressively and poignantly than before, and her reinvention damns the patriarchal eye that fears and despises bodies of the diseased and of old(er) women.

Old(er) women suffer differently from old(er) men because female aging remains in American society what Susan Sontag called it in 1972, "a process of becoming obscene. . . . That old women are repulsive is one of the most profound esthetic and erotic feelings in our culture."[19] These "erotic feelings" are really thanatic, a kind of femicide or broadly sexual violence that, in regard to visual representation, absents old(er) women from the erotic arena and kills people's ability to imagine, let alone physically image, old(er) women with love. Although menopause is becoming a popular subject—Gail Sheehy's *The Silent Passage: Menopause* (1992) was a bestseller, and I've heard ads on rock radio in my gym about menopause therapy—fitness authoritarianism, cosmetic surgery, and hormone usage to "correct" dryness of skin and vagina loom as female imperatives, and menopause, which for Western women occurs at the median age of fifty, remains a powerful marker of aging.

While the onset of menstruation is an erotic passage, and American culture deems women erotically appealing for the next thirty-five to forty years of their lives, the process of menopause may initiate a woman into invisibility and extreme subhumanity. Menopause would become an erotic passage if people used their capacity to eroticize everything—and I see this as a gift, not a gratuitous banality—in order to overcome their fear of flesh that moves. To give eros is to give social security, for the erotic is necessary to psychic and spiritual survival.

Wilke provides erotic security in *INTRA-VENUS* by confronting and embracing flesh that has moved in an aging illness. A reclining nude in the series presents Wilke as erotic agent and object. She is a damaged Venus as in *S.O.S.*, this time damaged by cancer and its therapies. Intravenous tubes pierce her, and bandages cover the sites, above her buttocks, of a failed bone-marrow transplant. Her stomach is loose, and she is no longer the feminine ideal. "My body has gotten old," she said a little less than a month before the bone-marrow transplant, "up to 188 pounds, prednisone-swelled, striations, dark lines, marks from bone-marrow harvesting." While an art historian could cite Renaissance martyr paintings as sources, she could also understand Wilke's vulnerable Venus, twenty years ago as well as recently, as a warrior displaying wounds and as the dark goddess, Hecate at the crossroads of life and death. Wilke has called her work "curative" and "medicinal," and she has said that "focusing on the self gives me the fighting spirit that I need" and that "my art is about loving myself."[20] The *INTRA-VENUS* nude shows Wilke within—intra—the veins of Venus, a lust for living in the artist's blood.

Wilke maintained that lust in a hospital, an institution that incarcerates and disciplines bodies. Informed consent is not really informed, for patients do not know or understand all the procedures they will undergo when they sign themselves into a hospital. They give their consent in a stressed if not desperate situation, which is the hope that the institution can return them to health. Hospitals turn patients into the powerless in a space and time that are not erotic, for they cut off the patient from the pleasure of relationships, intimacy, and work. Wilke eroticized her circumstances and shot *INTRA-VENUS* in the hospital, so she became an activist rather than a victim.[21]

In the *INTRA-VENUS* reclining nude Wilke resuscitates the boneless look developed by Giorgione and Titian, so she makes herself, as usual,

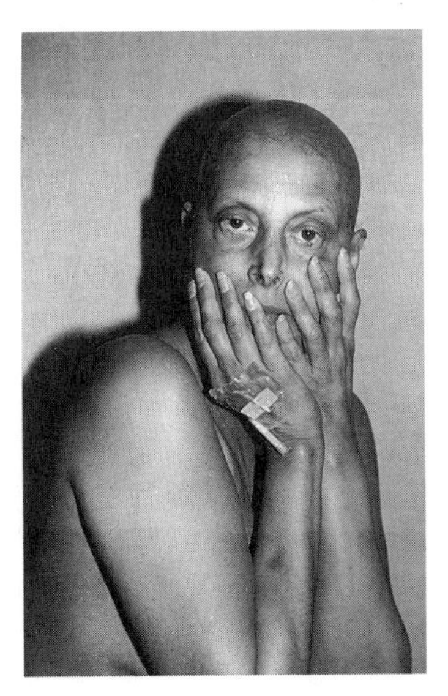

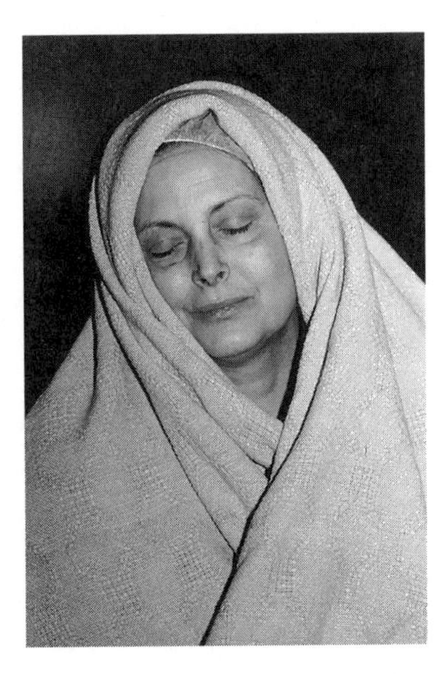

into a classical nude. But she is not female body as erotic trophy. This is because she—characteristically—proves that the body's boundaries are liminal and insecure—in *INTRA-VENUS*, through vivid and explicit pathos—and because, more than ever, she affirms, I AM WHO I AM. Bodily insecurity paradoxically becomes erotic social security, as does the ruin of the classical nude and of conventional femininity.

The erotic is not necessarily pretty. In *INTRA-VENUS* scars, bandages, baldness and unnaturally thin hair, and intravenous tubes signify pain. Wilke screams and stares. She crosses her arms over her stomach in self-protection, which feels sacred, a gesture of blessing, and she covers her head with a blue hospital blanket and closes her eyes in agonized and prayerful grace. As in *Hannah Wilke Super-T-Art*, where she poses as Mary and Christ, Wilke represents divine being in human being. Hail, Hannah, full of grace.

The erotic is beautiful rather than pretty. Femininity as a set of prettinesses, which are a set of limitations, reduces beauty to a weakness. Lakoff and Scherr say that society to some degree sees beautiful women's power as the power of the weak, because a beautiful woman's potency depends on others' perception of her appearance. She is captive to her beauty. A puritanical and simplistic feminism also sees women's beauty as a weakness. By concentrating on attacking the fashion, cosmetics, and plastic-surgery industries as exploitative and misogynist rather than developing transformative expansions of beauty, ascetic feminism keeps beauty's reductive definition: the beautiful woman is young—at the least, youthful—thin, and managed by "beauty" products and "beauty" services. It is that definition and not beauty itself that has oppressed women. Beauty is transformable because it is erotic, and the erotic refuses to be pinned down, for it is not a specimen. In human beings the erotic can be used to radicalize the human condition and to give pleasure that enriches and enlivens the world, often in unexpected ways.

One myth about feminine beauty is that it is dangerous. A beautiful woman is stunning, striking, a knockout, and a dangerous person is powerful. That power can be radically beneficial. Throughout her career Wilke performed the indispensable power of beauty and the soundness of danger. Beauty attracts, sometimes to such a degree that the viewer feels out of control, overcome by fear or sexual desire, by wonder and sheer enjoyment, or by a magic that disturbs her peace of mind. Beauty is departure from the ordinary, provoking and luring the viewer into uncommon thoughts and feelings. Wilke seduces her audience into terror and pain, the inescapability of death, the suffering behind the mask of lovely flesh, the "exotic" grace of change. To grow old gracefully is to go into erotic decline, to be the passive beauty who is losing her looks, while to be full of grace is to be at once dangerous and comforting.

Beauty can be dangerous to the status quo, especially when women deal with it, like Wilke, in both grave and playful ways. Society does not encourage women to "play with themselves," for sexual, political, intellectual, or creative pleasure. Obeying fashion's decrees is conformist and therefore highly restricted play, but making a spectacle of oneself may well be an assertion of erotic will. For spectacles do not have to follow orthodoxies. Woman-as-spectacle fascinates and disquiets many feminists, but Georgia O'Keeffe's nun- and monk-like "habits" and Louise Nevelson's ethnic butch/femme drag were a far cry from professional sex queens' regalia whose formulaic eroticism, for some feminists, calls into question the sex icon's erotic inventiveness. Wilke's self-display, which is erotic play, has always been an affront to proper femininity, which is patriarchy's containment of female possibility. Wilke as erotic spectacle verifies female genius.

Notes

Parts of this chapter were presented at the University of Arizona, Tucson, Arizona, March 1989.

Parts of this chapter appear in Joanna Frueh, Hannah Wilke, *ed. Thomas H. Kochheiser (Columbia: University of Missouri Press, 1989), 51–61; in Joanna Frueh, "Aesthetic and Postmenopausal Pleasures,"* M/E/A/N/I/N/G *14 (November 1993); and in Joanna Frueh, "The Erotic as Social Security,"* Art Journal *53 (Spring 1994). Material from* M/E/A/N/I/N/G *is reprinted by permission of* M/E/A/N/I/N/G: A Journal of Contemporary Art Issues, *and material from* Art Journal *is reprinted by permission of the College Art Association.*

1. Susan Brownmiller, *Femininity* (New York: Simon and Schuster, 1984), 24.
2. Una Stannard, "The Mask of Beauty," in Vivian Gornick and Barbara K. Moran, eds., *Woman in Sexist Society: Studies in Power and Powerlessness* (New York: Mentor, 1971), 187–203, and Naomi Wolf, *The Beauty Myth: How Images of Beauty Are Used Against Women* (New York: William Morrow, 1991).
3. Carolee Schneemann, in an interview with the author, 18 June 1992. Wilke first used "Venus envy" in a 1980 series of Polaroid photographs, and she spoke about Venus envy in conversation with the author, 9 June 1988.
4. Hannah Wilke, "Intercourse with . . . ," text for videotape performance, London Art Gallery, London, Ontario, Canada, 17 February 1977.
5. This and the quoted statements in the previous paragraph come from a conversation I had with Wilke on 9 June 1988.
6. Anne d'Harnoncourt and Walter Hopps, *Etant donnés: 1° la chute d'eau, 2° le gaz d'éclairage: Reflections on a New Work by Marcel Duchamp* (Philadelphia: Phildelphia Museum of Art, 1973), 64.
7. Hannah Wilke in conversation with the author, 9 June 1988.
8. Marcel Duchamp in Pierre Cabanne, *Dialogues with Marcel Duchamp*, trans. Ron Padgett (New York: Viking, 1971), 88.
9. Hannah Wilke in conversation with the author, 9 June 1988.
10. Robin Lakoff and Raquel L. Scherr, *Face Value: The Politics of Beauty* (Boston: Routledge and Kegan Paul, 1984), 14–15.
11. Brownmiller, *Femininity*, 18.
12. Lois Banner, *American Beauty* (New York: Alfred A. Knopf, 1983), 3.
13. Hannah Wilke in Chris Huestis and Marvin Jones, "Hannah Wilke: Hannah Wilke's Art, Politics, Religion and Feminism," *The New Common Good* (May 1985): 9.
14. Lucy R. Lippard, *From the Center: Feminist Essays on Women's Art* (New York: E. P. Dutton, 1976), 126.
15. Barbara G. Walker, *The Woman's Encyclopedia of Myths and Secrets* (San Francisco: Harper and Row, 1983), 350–51
16. See chapter 2, "No Rite of Passage," and chapter 17, "Serenity and Power," in Germaine Greer, *The Change: Women, Aging and the Menopause* (New York: Alfred A. Knopf, 1992).

17. Wilke used the phrase "beauty to beast" regarding her appearance in conversation with the author in early June 1992.
18. Laura Mulvey, "Visual Pleasure and Narrative Cinema," *Screen* 16 (Autumn 1975): 6–18.
19. Susan Sontag, "The Double Standard of Aging," *Saturday Review* (23 September 1972): 37.
20. All Wilke's statements about her illness and *INTRA-VENUS* are from telephone conversations with the author, 11 May 1992 and 9 January 1993.
21. Linda Singer's "Hospitalization and AIDS," in Linda Singer, *Erotic Welfare: Sexual Theory and Politics in the Age of Epidemic*, ed. and introduced by Judith Butler and Maureen MacGrogan (London: Routledge, 1993), 100–107, informed my thinking about hospitals and Wilke's art.

PART THREE

Loving Stories

RHETORIC AS CANON

[*A short, tight, black bouclé sweater draws attention to Frueh's skin, because the audience can see it through the knit, except for the area her black bra covers. Also, below the jewel neckline, three cut-out scallop shapes edged in bluish-silver sequins bare much of Frueh's chest. Cap sleeves emphasize the muscles of her upper arms. A knee-length gabardine skirt, suede slingback high heels, and velvet headband, all black, complete the decorous and seductive costume.*]

She sees no beginning. She sees no end. One is a false start, the other an unfitting conclusion. She sees no background. She sees no foreground. Between these deceptive horizons a middleground exists, always changing, never middle-of-the-road.[1]

I said I saw the wind and she didn't believe me. My first-grade teacher's point, that I be empirically accurate, denied the conflation of senses and of senses and thought that is experience, while also negating the fact that communication about events and objects can be poetically precise.

Years ago, after reading an article of mine, a colleague said, "This is more like fiction than criticism." I asked, "What's the difference?"

Both women wanted me, the teller, to be an observer of truth, to exist outside it, to practice a prescribed method.

Since the 1980s, when critical theory inundated the art world and informed the work of many artists, art critics, and art historians, it has become—certainly in theory—impossible to tell the truth. Language, we have learned, is a cultural construct, which means it is none of the following: neutral, transparent, absolute as a conveyer of the universal or the true.

In art, feminists and other revisionists have proved terminology—greatness; major/minor; master; the father of expressionism; the heroes of modern art; the war-and-miracles vocabulary of divine creativity, glories and triumphs, conquests and battles—to be vehicles of masculinist ideology.

Language—figures of speech and the telling structures into which they fit—is no longer comfortable. At once controlling and arbitrary, the old ways of art-critical and -historical writing and speaking, which are both storytelling, should embarrass any well-read and well-meaning postmodernist.

A former colleague wanted to engage me in argument. "Art historians like to be right," he said. "Don't you want to argue?"

"No," I replied.

Although many of us understand that the method of storytelling shapes the objects and events about which it speaks, that a dominant method functions through its repression of other methods, and that, to paraphrase Hélène Cixous, political liberation is unimaginable without linguistic liberation, we continue to use a canon of rhetoric structured by supposed order and consensus regarding clarity, closure, professionalism, and academic responsibility. At worst, an army of art voices has conquered and cleansed art itself to a modernist purity, a bland and universal rhetoric of the White, the West, and Man.

"The history of art will become sterile unless it is constantly enriched by a close contact with the study of man."[2] So wrote an illustrious art historian. But the study of man and the studies conducted under the direction and rhetoric of manly thinking have made art history and criticism sterile.

• • •

Penelope, unweaving every night, to save herself from unwanted men.
text, from the Latin *textus*, past participle of *textere*, to weave

Storytellers, seriously taken by standard texts and by where to draw the line, keep the order. Lip service notwithstanding, they do not break the peace arranged by the order of ancient arguments. Taken in, taken over, they take for granted their own aphasia. Feminist art historians and critics, too:

> Submerged . . . once again in a slightly reformed but still traditional notion of history. . . . So perhaps inevitably their initially admirable intentions are ultimately betrayed by academic conservatism and defensiveness. . . . A radical reform, if not a total deconstruction of the present structure of the discipline is needed.
>
> We are witnessing a paradigm shift which will rewrite all cultural history.[3]

I play with words that I respect, by Griselda Pollock in the second statement and by her and Roszika Parker in the first. They critique the power plays—cultural, ideological, and economic—that govern the state of art. I hear the old refrain of revolution and I read reformist prose, argumentation that diminishes a difference in content because the paradigm of art storytelling has not shifted in form.

Why not de-scribe, un-write, rather than rewrite, which sounds like the broken record of so-called revolution?

I've been using *storytelling* to stand for a range of related words and to convey several meanings. Storytelling is: a rich and ancient skill, and the word also suggests that its practitioner is a liar. Fiction writers tell stories, as do historians. Neither is truer. Neither makes more sense than the other, since measuring truth through manner of speaking is absurd. A story is simply the telling of a connected series of events and concepts for the purpose of informing or entertaining. Storytelling is narrative, which may be argumentation, a process of arriving at reasons and conclusions; discourse, written or spoken; and rhetoric, skill in the effective use of speech, principles and rules of composition first formulated by the ancient Greeks. Much contemporary discourse analysis reiterates principles of ancient rhetoric. Storytelling also partakes of orality, text, and oratory.

I heard she didn't get the job because they said she was a poet, not a historian.

• • •

In poetry the word may tell unheard-of stories, for it may announce the abnormal thinker whose words, with luck and tenacity, may take on velocity and magnitude.[4]

The artist Stamos asked me, "Do you go to openings? You must. That's where you hear things, where you get informed."

Gossip. Hearsay. I hear, and I say to you that stories must be told in the line of battle with the powers that be.

Art storytelling is a disagreeable agreement with authority. This rhetoric of supposed consensus includes a basis in scientific and apodictic method and a belief in the Cartesian notion that I think, therefore I am. The voice of reason censors the teller, disciplining his story into a structure of descriptive realism that does not permit play, that separates form and content in the name of uni-formity, that upholds the destructive principle of mind over matter.

The still universal sway of reason in academic writing justifies itself through tradition and habit, which are strict. The voice of reason enforces linear progression, the perfectly woven tale, seamless, of smooth texture.

As a sophomore in high school I had to take a speech class. After I made a presentation the teacher said, "Don't use your hands when you speak."

No body.

It is abnormal for the body to speak its mind. But the sentient body is also the conscious intellect ever ready to let itself go—to engage ideas erotically, to be nourished and nauseated by thinking, which is everything that the soul-inseparable-from-the-body does.[5]

[*Frueh works herself into a subtle lamentation.*]

The rip, the hole, the patch, the unmatched inharmonious threads, the stitches out of line, the threadbare spot that moans, the stain that whispers revelry cannot contribute to art storytelling as a picture of reality that is only an illusion of reality that easily acquires greater authority than the actuality it describes.

A review in *Art in America*, say the artists, is worth more than crowds of people coming to see my work.

Of course audience and context for the words account in large measure for such a belief, but the combination of context and a description of the art decorated with some interpretation and analysis that hone the picture in words create a valued hyperreality that few challenge as escape into a cosmetic tidiness.

cosmetic, from the Greek *kosmetikos,* skilled in arranging, *kosmein,* to arrange, adorn, *kosmos,* order

The pretty pictures, which are the seamless stories told in art history and criticism, seek to arrange an order where the teller shares in the transcendent ego of an intellectual community whose members are bearers of truth. This is a frightening utopia, where all subjects speak as one through form, even though they seem to speak differently through the foregrounding of content and the use of style.

I read this to myself. I fear its seamlessness. Have I masked my scars and wrinkles? Arranged yet another cosmetic text? Is there a difference between seamless argument and compositional and aesthetic skill?

I accuse myself. I should change and cancel my own arguments, de-scribe my own positions. The most erotic positions never suit a pontificator, who, pontiff of art, can speak only in one voice, which is the preaching of official authority.

The statement and proof of the case were, according to Aristotle, the two essential elements of a speech, though he said orators also provided an introduction and conclusion. The same story, over and over. Statement and proof alternate or succeed one another as a series of ideas and images arranged progressively, in a neat and reasonable order, to make the point, which is to reach the climax. Coming to a conclusion.

O come all ye faithful.

The words come like a river or like waves. This process, predictable only in its unexpectedness and [the girl's] sense that she was both drifting and propelled, had entertained her since she was little. In high school she named the process the liquid world of words, and she decided that the liquid world brought her messages from the soul-and-mind-inseparable-from-the-body.[6]

• • •

Since the early 1980s, the idea of writing the body, first elaborated by some French feminists, has fascinated me. But all along I've wondered, How does anyone write the body, not simply convey "carnal knowing" but embed that in words?[7]

anti-thesis
coming apart at the seams

A man from Montana read his poem about a flamenco dancer he saw perform in Santa Fe. She was so hot-blooded, so beautiful in her fifties and her discipline that he did not sleep for days. These are my words, not his, for his did not match the passion she had inspired in him. I imagined her dancing till her rhythms, so strict, seemed crazy, dancing till her tongue could hang out, stick out like the Gorgon Medusa's. Warding off evil, dancing delirium while knowing every move.

The good story of Hollywood movies corresponds to the good-sex stereotype of male performance: beginning (foreplay), middle (intercourse), and end (climax). That story is pleasure with play seriously legislated and limited by structure.

The girl pulled her menstrual pad to one side and dipped two fingers into her blood. Forcing herself, because she was doing something she had neither read nor talked to anyone about, and seducing herself with the pleasure of knowledge through sensation, she licked the fluid from her fingers. It tasted like blood from a cut, but the flavor was denser, the texture thicker. Part of her felt that this act was nothing unusual, that it had been nothing to fear, so she did it again. As she repeated the dipping and licking, a feeling earlier submerged by her sense of the ordinary overwhelmed her.

Words tumbled over one another, waves that seemed to knock the wind out of her like imagined breakers that would swell, then draw her underwater, groin first.

The words in her mind, made by her lips with no sound, went on and on, impossible to remember later. Arms around her knees, rocking back and forth, then side to side, she listened to the language brought by her blood, the liquid world of words.[8]

• • •

Deny erotic urge and urgency and the speaker becomes diseased. Never mistake his rabidness for passion: pontiffs can foam at the mouth, but they can never come as they speak.

We see women artists being the subjects and producers of culture. Using visual rhetoric invented by men, such as the female nude, to emancipate it. Diving deep into the masculine womb and surfacing: Carolee Schneemann the magic ground for snakes, the voice of fearless sex; Nancy Spero turning the dead into joyous athletes, laughing battalions: Rachel Rosenthal baring age and nakedness; Joan Semmel staring without being a voyeur; Bailey Doogan depicting what she has named the angry aging bitch. We know the power of images and the importance of transforming them.

In art storytelling, one way to invent the terrorist texts, abnormal discourse, and ecstatic espionage discussed by Patricia Yaeger in *Honey-Mad Women: Emancipatory Strategies in Women's Writing*, her examination of women novelists' work and play with storytelling, is to establish an emancipatory relation to the dominant tradition.[9] One where the subject speaks for herself.

For the teller of the good story is not entirely present. Control personal pronouns, parenthetical intrusions, signs of the teller's difference from the text, her unseamed stories, unseemly voice.

Liquidate the speaker in the flow of reason.

And, rather than operating only from a position of silence and absence or, at best, constraint—because we all speak the patriarchal language, which, according to some feminists, severely alienates women from their own experience—women writers, posits Yaeger, have also been honey-mad for speech.[10]

The pontiff must learn to sweeten her tongue.

Even style does not wholly distinguish or amplify the voice, and neither does wordplay. The latter may interrupt structure to some degree by jumping out of the bounds of reason, but the good story's arrangement ties the tongue. Style, although it fleshes out an argument, is still adornment. Style itself cannot be full-bodied, that is, full-voiced.

Dressed in style, I think, therefore I am. In the u-topia, the no-place that grants independence from the body to the mind. I think, therefore I am. No-body.

Art rhetoric betrays matter—the physical, the body, the art object, the sens-ible—by speaking mind to mind, so that only the mind matters.

"We're creatures of the margins," said Gordon, my father-in-law. Gordon was noting how human beings belong to both nature and culture. So we should not feel torn between the two.

I liked his use of the word *margins,* but I also thought about the word *marginal* being used *ad nauseam* in the art world.

Liminal seems a more useful word than *marginal,* for then one condition blends into another.

[*Frueh takes a deep and silent breath.*]

I am nature and culture, mind soul body, scholar and gossip, poet, historian, teller and tale, ranter and rationalist, performer and performance, the oral, the oratory, the oracular, the figure of speech.

Notes

"Rhetoric as Canon" is a revision of a paper with the same title delivered on the "Open Session" panel at the 1991 College Art Association Conference in Washington, D.C. Many thanks to the panel's moderator, Mary D. Garrard, for her comments and suggestions, which strengthened the paper for presentation.

A version of this chapter appeared in the New Art Examiner *18 (June/Summer 1991). That material is reprinted by permission of the* New Art Examiner.

1. Joanna Frueh, "Desert City" (unpublished novel, 1988), 1.
2. E. H. Gombrich, *Art and Illusion: A Study in the Psychology of Pictorial Representation* (Princeton: Princeton University Press, 1969), x.
3. Roszika Parker and Griselda Pollock, *Old Mistresses: Women, Art and Ideology* (New York: Pantheon, 1981), 45–48, and Griselda Pollock, *Vision and Difference: Femininity, Feminism and the Histories of Art* (London: Routledge, 1988), 17.
4. Patricia Yaeger, *Honey-Mad Women: Emancipatory Strategies in Women's Writing* (New York: Columbia University Press, 1988), 39, writes that in poetry a word may serve "as vector, as harbinger of an abnormal way of thinking."
5. Margaret Miles's term "carnal knowing" is relevant to thinking about body/mind unity. Miles, *Carnal Knowing: Female Nakedness and Religious Meaning in the Christian West* (Boston: Beacon, 1989), 8–9, writes, "'Carnal knowing' refers to an activity in which the intimate interdependence and irreducible cooperation of thinking, feeling, sensing, and understanding is revealed. . . . The consanguinity of human beings depends on mutual recognition of the common bond of a sentient body, whose most vivid experiences create consciousness."

6. Adapted from Frueh, "Desert City," 6–7.
7. I use Margaret Miles's term.
8. Adapted from Frueh, "Desert City," 16–17.
9. "Terrorist text," "abnormal discourse," and "ecstatic espionage" are phrases and ideas that recur throughout Yaeger, *Honey-Mad Women.*
10. See Yaeger, *Honey-Mad Women,* especially chapter 1.

JEEZ LOUISE

[Frueh's clothes correspond to the colors of Louise Bourgeois's marble sculptures: white, black, and pink. Before Frueh begins, the audience sees her walk to the podium in a white gabardine skirt and sheer white stockings, a black wool jacket, buttoned to the bottom of her throat and fitted at the waist, and black suede pumps. She reads a list of Louise Bourgeois's works as if it were a poem. A slide of each work appears on a screen as Frueh says the title.]

Louise Bourgeois at age one, Paris, 1913
Femme-Maison (Woman House)
Observer
The Blind Leading the Blind
He Disappeared into Complete Silence (one of nine engravings with text)
Brother and Sister
Sleeping Figure
Untitled
Femme Volage (Fickle Woman)
Spiral Women

Figures
Spiral/Summer
Labyrinthine Tower
Lair
The Quartered One
Germinal
Fillette
Colonnata
Hanging Janus
Harmless Woman
Cumul I
Femme Couteau (Knife Woman)
Eye to Eye
Untitled
The Destruction of the Father, detail
Maisons Fragiles/Empty Houses
A Banquet/A Fashion Show of Body Parts
Partial Recall, detail
Femme-Maison
Fallen Woman
Femme Couteau
Female Portrait
Shredder
Femme Maison
Nature Study: Pink Fountain
Nature Study
Nature Study
Spiral Woman
Nature Study
Nature Study
Untitled (Fingers)
Lair
Nature Study
Louise Bourgeois at age 71

[*Frueh says, "Projector off, please, and lights up." Then she unbuttons her jacket, slips it off, and lays it on a stool to her left. She wears a pale-pink camisole with spaghetti straps and a pearl necklace that hangs to her breasts.*]

Criticism

In her introduction to the catalogue for a recent Bourgeois exhibition which originated at Cincinnati's Taft Museum, Ruth Meyer, director of the Taft, says, regarding Stuart Morgan's essays on Bourgeois, "Morgan assumes that we have a superficial knowledge of [Bourgeois's] career, and so he takes us well beyond a conventional recitation of events. For an artist like Bourgeois, whose art is a visual autobiography, this approach is the most appropriate."[1]

[*Frueh's desire is that the audience will hear other critics' words and hers as a kind of call-and-response.*]

Morgan himself writes that Bourgeois's "'say,' her repeated proof that she would not be eliminated, was her art . . . , a body of work . . . which confirmed, time after time, that it *was* her: her circumstances, her emotions, her flesh, her sexuality."[2]

If Bourgeois's art *is* her, then mustn't the critic's writing be her, the critic? Mustn't visual autobiography provoke critical autobiography, a leap beyond the plateaus of critical decency—which is simply convention—a stride off a cliff, into indecent exposure?

And as the critic leaps she climbs, out of the morass of the appropriate into the complex clarity of the truly fitting. There the critic learns her voice, has her say, knows she belongs to the living body that is the home, the homeostasis of artist and critic.

Morgan believes, "Duchamp's remark that the spectator completes the work of art has never been truer than in the case of Bourgeois's sculptures."[3]

If this is true, then the critic-spectator, at home in the One Body of art and criticism, creates a discourse that is as much about her as it is about Bourgeois. To complete is to make whole or perfect. Incomplete discourse denies the critic's self, both her life and human life as personal passage, which an artist such as Bourgeois reveals.

"Crossing barriers," Morgan writes, "the loss of strict limits, is as familiar in Bourgeois's work as her own signature."[4]

The signature of standard criticism is its stricture, the unspoken rules that obviate against the critic having his say, the familiar limitations of forced and false objectivity, of the tight-assed essay, that barricade the critic's life from the artist's. This is a loss, but the situation is familiar, so we notice nothing. We ourselves as readers are the lost, and we don't even know it.

One purpose of criticism is to uncover, not only the artist's relationship to us, but also the fact that we are in relationship *with* the artist as we recognize her in her work.

Uncover, unveil, undress, expose, reveal; cross over, under, around and through; tear down, tear up, tear off, tear away: terror.

I had written a review for *Artforum,* in 1979, on Nicholas Africano's paintings. The editor in charge of reviews asked for revisions. Too much about life, she said, not enough art. Funny, I thought, this is precisely the problem with art criticism: too much art, not enough life. For art critics, concentrated on art—as style, history, innovation, influence—suck at the artist's heart but take too little nourishment from the lifeblood. I see such nourishment as mutual transfusion, the simultaneous vivification of art and criticism. As things stand, critics are negatively vampiric and thankless.

Hardening my heart, the borders that would shield the most vulnerable frontiers, the interior that loves Bourgeois's work because it penetrates protection, I took some of the life out of the Africano review, and it was published.

William Rubin, director emeritus of the Department of Painting and Sculpture at New York's Museum of Modern Art, describes Bourgeois's work as "psychic poetry."[5]

Taking the life out of criticism reduces its potential, the psychic poetry that flows, spurts, floats, erupts within the critic and that could be grounded in critical texts as poetics. The interior of art and criticism, which is the Land of One Body, the heart of light and darkness, the seeming extremes of knowledge and the unknown, is the home of both the psyche, as soul, self, and mind, and of Psyche herself. Here, in your and my and Bourgeois's interior, Psyche lives, as symbol of the search for love.

In Greco-Roman mythology, the maiden Psyche fell in love with Eros, god of love, but had to undergo trials in order to be with him. The maiden's journey, the maiden voyage: the search for love is always an initiation, the defloration of some virginity.

. . .

Deborah Wye, curator of the Museum of Modern Art's 1982 Bourgeois retrospective, writes that Bourgeois's "works invite private encounters that engender responses on both visceral and imaginary levels."[6]

Bourgeois is the visceral and imaginative virgin, continually re-deflowering herself through the recurrent yet changing thematic and formal patterns of her art. Such re-defloration is a redefining of the self, a transfusion of essence and transformation to the critic as visceral and imaginative virgin.

Frida Kahlo's double self-portrait *The Two Fridas* depicts a blood transfusion between her selves. One of many ways to read this painting is as an image of sisterly love, a metaphoric exchange of the substance of survival itself. Sisterly love is feminist, and critics generally see Bourgeois's art as feminist. Thus the virgin critic and Louise exist as sisters, and art criticism becomes a manifestation of kinship. In her private encounters and public say, the critic comes home. Also, because feminist relatives are such through blood or affinity, brotherly love can be feminist. Sisters together, brothers together, brother and sister together can transfuse each other. Blood sisters and blood brothers share the psychic quest.

Wye says that by 1978 "Bourgeois had worked in [a] personal, idiosyncratic, and expressionist mode for over forty years."[7]

Intimacy is the modus operandi of the artist and her critic.

"Fundamental to [Bourgeois's] character as an artist," Wye explains, "is the struggle of an individual actively attempting to define herself through her art—to understand, control, and express herself through the discovery and exploration of specific imagery."[8]

The house, the body: two sites of home. Female and male: more conjunctive imagery, and it defines our deepest natures, one absolute home as multi-gendered and intensely, beautifully, and terrifyingly sexed.

The critic who struggles for self-understanding, -control, and -expression, who attempts to define himself through Bourgeois and Bourgeois through him, is snared by both his own and Bourgeois's imagery, separate yet fused housings of passion, pain, and pleasure.

• • •

Bourgeois says, "When you experience pain, you can withdraw and protect yourself. But the security of the lair can also be a trap."[9]

Wild animals rest in their lairs.

My lover climbs rocks. The mountain is his lair, protection from painful change, from realizing commitment rather than simply believing in it.

The critic seeks refuge too, in conventional criticism. The critic is caught in his own trap of protection—the essay, lecture, podium, projector, history, slides, jargon, costume—the trappings of art scholarship.

Climbers use what they call protection—metal tools that secure the rope.

Slides are fools' tools.

Most art critics live in a fool's paradise, the perfect state of protection, the creation of a mistaken harmony between art and critic, which is the outworn tune of object and objectifier.

Lovers are both objects and objectifiers, but they sing a different melody. They croon, I am a fool for you. This is because they are wild, for each other.

My lover writes,

> It seems so natural that I forget that no one before has been able to take my passion. They have asked for, I don't know, "a cultured approach." I feel music I see your face my arm is in pain pushing the pen to your paper I wish it was your hair your hips your eyes deep set in mine deep in me   I want you deep in me. Take me   Deep in me   Take me   Deep in.[10]

I think about wild critics and wild lovers, both of whom must climb and go deep, and I hear the lyrics:

> Wild thing you make my heart sing
> You make my brain ring
> You make my cunt sting
> Wild thing, I think you move me
> But I want to know for sure
> I love you[11]

Extremes and Equilibrium

Critics write about isolation and relationship in Bourgeois's art, her focus on solitary and massed forms. Self and others, solitude and community: the critic dissolves the distance between the two terms, for she orchestrates and improvises a harmony between private speech and public hearing.

The critic creates an equation that dissolves the difference between object and objectifier. The equilibration of isolated and communal selves meeting in grace and passion produces the love-making between me and Russell, or a love-making statement such as critic Arlene Raven's "I enter Harmony Hammond's work."[12] Mutual entry and enteredness join lovers, join art and critic, so that each pair enters into community.

Such entry can serve as a catalyst for entrancement. Catalysis derives from the Greek *k-a-t-a-l-y-s-i-s*, dissolution. Entrancement is the dissolution of separateness, the release for the critic to experience the extremes in Bourgeois's art and in his own life.

I spell out *k-a-t-a-l-y-s-i-s*, I make it clear. (Russell writes, Send me your l-e-t-t-e-r-s of love.)[13] I spill out as I spell. Louise spills her guts as she casts the spell of extremes—damage and healing, the soothing and the violent, the refined and the raw, vulnerability and power.

Spellbound between extremes, the critic finds her own balance.

Balance is extreme entrancement, the purity of clairvoyance, clear sight.

Critic Donald Kuspit says that Bourgeois "is not afraid to make what can only be called 'defecatory sculpture.'"[14]

To defecate is to clear the body, to discharge impurities. The artist and her critic get their shit out, come clean. The cleansing regulates the unconscious and creates homeostasis, a peace between artist and critic.

Louise explains, "Janus . . . is a reference to the kind of polarity we represent. . . . The polarity I experience is a drive toward extreme violence and revolt . . . and a retiring, I wouldn't say passivity . . . but a need for peace, a complete peace with the self, with others, with the environment."[15]

Janus is the two-faced god who sees the future and the past. Are the gods engaged in double-dealing when we human beings cannot make peace with the present because we take after Janus and are geared too much in both our memories and our tomorrows?

Russell and I were walking a trail at Cochise Stronghold, less than two hours out of Tucson. In that place Cochise made his last stand. (The present is inevitable, though our society denies this.) I had led the way up, mostly at a maniacal pace. Midway down I stopped, turned, and said, "Russell, this is the walk of no mercy. We need to stop." We laughed. Then we sat, I in the middle of the trail. We knew we were in dire straits with one another. I crossed my legs and said, "I'm exhausted from moving so fast." The speed of our love was frightening. Though we desired what he called "the relationship of eternity," ours, it terrified him. "I'm sitting here," I said, "and I feel like I can't go back and I can't go forward."

[*Frueh pauses longer than usual, for the memory of Cochise Stronghold is exhausting.*]

My feelings were in a state of extreme violence, and yet I felt like retiring. Was I in stasis or a strange balance or at the beginning of one more leg of the Janus journey—peace through extremes?

Bourgeois uses pink and white and black marble, colors of skin. I'm especially taken by the pink and black, vulnerability and power. I'm struggling to balance them, and in my struggle I'm attracted also by some of her sculptures' poignantly smooth surfaces and contours, their hardness and roughness too; by the limp yet tumescent shapes; by the discreteness of form on the one hand, the sense of something in formation on the other; by the simultaneously tender yet stoic groups of forms and figures; by the beauty of stability and flux; by the frankness and silence of art.

I called my friend Peggy. I said, "I can't stay with Russell anymore. Can I stay with you?" She said, "You sound like you're *in extremis*." I said, "I am."

Some of Louise's sculptures spiral and suggest to me, in my struggle, labyrinthine turmoil, the psyche twisting in on itself, or perhaps in the process of untwisting coiled tension. I want to remember others of her sculptures as solely soothing, because of their fluent contours, but memory does not prove accurate. Nonetheless, I look to Louise for solace, wish to see her as a soothsayer so I can find in her art a resolution of my own extremes.

The Body

In Louise's *Femme Maison* drawings and paintings, a house is a naked woman's head, sometimes her head and torso both. The works are merciless.

The woman must be claustrophobic. As the ironic homebody, she is walled up, boxed in, so uncomfortably housed that she has no home.

I wonder if I am homeless like the *femme maison*, only homebound in my obsessive thoughts of a shared and loving environment with Russell. Or am I truly heading homeward, to the "uncultured" comforts he and I have imagined together?

On the endpapers in a Bourgeois book are columns of one phrase handwritten in red: "*je t'aime*."[16]

God, love gets corny. Home *is* where the heart is. A house is not a home unless it is the embodiment of love.

"Bourgeois's relation to her work," says Morgan, "is direct and unforced. 'I feel that I have been shredded,' she tells a reporter."[17]

Louise's anger, pain, and insecurity regarding her father's lover, the tutor of English for the three Bourgeois children, is a tale of shredding.

We are all shredded by love.

Louise and Russell try to kill the father. He writes me, "I wonder if I am insane. Such hurt. Such inability to let go of what is important, loving, intelligent, and powerful in your life. For most people killing a father is a matter of course, of living."[18] But for Russell it is not, for his father, at a distance of emotion and miles, has been Russell's major commitment since his parents were divorced when he was seven.

Louise's story, told in relation to *The Destruction of the Father*, is gruesome and satisfying. He would hold forth at dinner night after night. She fantasized that the family pulled him onto the table, dismembered and devoured him.

The Destruction of the Father is aesthetic reification, a way to get nourishment from the father.

Russell and I share a vision of tearing each other apart as we make love. It is a reenactment, altered through our passion, of ancient fertility rituals in which men were sacrificed, ripped to pieces.

Blood sister and blood brother.

We are all fed by love.

Louise's mother was a figure of love, of comfort, order, and calm, of nurturance embodied. I think of the many-breasted Diana of Ephesus.

Louise's performance, presented in conjunction with her installation piece *Confrontation*, is called *A Banquet/A Fashion Show of Body Parts*. Both men and women wear costumes whose protruding forms suggest breasts and penises. They are all Diana of Ephesus. They are all female and male. They all represent the body as feast. They are all more than enough.

Love is more than enough, yet never enough.

Darling Russell, we gorge, then starve. Where is the balance between survival and celebration?

I look at the *femme couteau*s, female bodies as knives, as frightened and frightening, as powerful in their vulnerability. Perhaps this is the answer: to combine apparent extremes rather than moving away from them toward an unhappy medium.

I see *medium* as a synonym for *lukewarm*.

But to be frightened and frightening, full of power and vulnerability, is to be the medium, like Louise, of survival and celebration.

From the mediumistic perspective we see that, as Louise says, "It seems rather evident . . . that our own body is a figuration that appears in Mother Earth."[19]

Louise creates at once physical and metaphysical configurations, the body as father and as mother, as hard and heavy and rocky as earth, rooted in groups like trees in a forest, smooth as placid water, hanging, like the unidentifiable corpse of a fruit or animal, austere like Arizona mesas, abundant, the way untampered-with earth can be.

The Bourgeois Body

To be bourgeois is to be a philistine, domesticated by material and mundane concerns. The critic must seek a different definition of *bourgeois* if she wishes to apply the term to Louise's art. For, as critic Robert Storr writes, "Bourgeois is rivaled only by Giacometti in the making of 'disagreeable,' undomesticatable objects."[20]

A bourgeois was a freeman of a city, as distinguished from a peasant or a gentleman. A bourgeois was between the two, a member of the middle class. The Bourgeois Body is between extremes, a reconciliation that results in freedom: the undomesticated and therefore free-"men"/free-"women" we see in Louise's sculptures.

[*Frueh coaxes, the way one talks to a lover when one is desperate for response.*]

What about you, Russell, and me? Are we like the Bourgeois Body, a free-man and a free-woman, reconciled to a multiplicity of genders, to the terror and beauty of being sexed? Are we free, falling bodies? Are we fallen, in love, suspended and utterly vulnerable, already subjected to the psychic harm reflected in some of Bourgeois's work as abstracted bodily injury?

Lucy R. Lippard quotes Bourgeois: "We are all vulnerable in some way, and we are all male-female."[21]

You invited me out to dinner, Russell, our first date, as we lovingly joke about it now. And you asked me, "Am I a man?" I instantly answered, "As much as I'm a woman."

Your question amazed me, penetrated my protection, embraced my vulnerability.

Already we were deep in, beyond the borders of gender, like the Bourgeois Body.

Russell writes to me,

Your letter—your "scrutiny,"
Your watching me on the hood of the car
Makes me wet
And
Who's to say it doesn't
My guts are
Wet
For what you saw in me
The stuff
Stuff
That I don't see and can't control and
Is out of control
Which—is—
The essence of me
The essence of wet.[22]
[*Frueh sighs.*]

Dire Straits

Wye says that Bourgeois's "work, in some way, takes the form of a strategy for survival."[23]

The critic sees her sister, who is almost twice her age, in dire straits, a pain that, at the risk of psychic harm, forces clarity to surface.

The critic sees her sister sailing through Scylla and Charybdis, her works of art the signs of wounds and bruisings, the aesthetic scars of experience.

My friend Marla says she loves the scars on people's flesh. They are signs of life.

My legs were bruised all summer, from causes that I could not conclude were external.

I climbed with Russell, banged my shin on a rock, may bear the scar.

Louise says about *The Destruction of the Father*, "It is a very murderous piece, an impulse that comes when one is under too much stress and one turns against those one loves the most."[24]

I address Russell in a note I keep for myself:

You wanted everything, you got it and now you're an asshole. You say you've asked of life to see a lot, but not for the best. You don't want the best you can have? What can I say to you? What will you be able to hear? You're acting like your father. The disappearing act. You say this is involuntary. I understand needing time, space, requirements for the self. But disappearing acts are cruelties to the people who love and are loved by the disappeared. For in some sense the disappeared are the dead—to part of themselves and to others. The disappeared, emotionally, are political prisoners, captive to their pasts and patterns.

Love does free.

Louise knows about love, the magical depth of the unconscious, which she uses in her art. She says, "The unconscious is something which is volcanic in tone and yet you cannot do anything about it. You had better be its friend, or accept it, or love it if you can, because it might get the better of you. You never know."[25]

I dreamed my house had three front doors, one behind the other. It was night and I was afraid I hadn't locked them. I checked, and I was right. But I left them as they were.

I woke up terrified long before dawn.

In the morning, though, I was glad I'd chosen to keep the doors open.

Morgan notes "the state of reverie which [Bourgeois's] sculpture demands."[26]

I've spent much time lost, and found, in reverie about Louise, about the dream of three open doors, about Russell. *Reverie* derives from the Middle French for delirium. Delirium can be craziness, but I have been nowhere near crazy. No nearer or farther than usual. I have been in deep pain. Coffee drunk in familiar places has helped heal me. I have not deadened myself. I am fully alive, amazed I did not even wish for numbness. Living, being alive works the pain through more quickly than does paralysis. Reverie brings revelation.

Revelations are simply articulated. It is the complexity of their truth that is overwhelming. Louise's sculptures are revelations. Although they are related to Minimalism, in simplicity and directness of presence and sensation, Louise's work has more heart and a different wisdom. It is the entrancement with extremes that separates her. The balancing results in lucid and simple forms on which the critic can focus for comfort. Comfort comes from the objects' frankness, the obvious assertion of sheer existence.

Pre-Raphaelite poet and painter Dante Gabriel Rossetti put it this way:

> The wind flapped loose, the wind was still,
> Shaken out dead from tree and hill:
> I had walked on at the wind's will,—
> I sat now, for the wind was still.[27]

[*Frueh finds herself reading more lightly, slowly, and melodiously as the poem progresses, as if she must again—for she has read and thought about this poem countless times—picture herself as the poem's I. The experience is succinct—all those one-syllable words—and prolongedly sad and revelatory.*]

> Between my knees my forehead was,—
> My lips, drawn in, said not Alas!
> My hair was over in the grass,
> My naked ears heard the day pass.
> My eyes, wide open, had the run
> Of some ten weeds to fix upon;
> Among those few, out of the sun,
> The woodspurge flowered, three cups in one.
>
> From perfect grief there need not be
> Wisdom or even memory:
> One thing then learnt remains to me,—
> The woodspurge has a cup of three.[28]

My friend Edith tells me that in gematria, the cabalistic method of explaining the Hebrew Scriptures by means of the cryptographic significance of the words, *trial* and *miracle* are the same number.

Jeez Louise

Jerry Gorovoy, who has worked as Louise's assistant, writes, in a reverie on Louise's art, "The feelings of fear, helplessness, ambivalent eroticism, isolation, and hostility which inform the anxiety of human relations are the forces which drive the individual to a radical reinvention of reality."[29]

We invent our lives. We are our own fictions, created with imagination, dreamed into reality with love as well as the feelings Gorovoy lists.

The artist and her critic are radicals, dealing with extremes to reinvent themselves in their work. The reinvention is terror and delirium.

Oh, Jeez, Louise, I've lost my mind and my knees.

For I am falling. I can't get a grip on myself. I'm drunk, stoned, drifting, dreaming, raving. I'm ecstatic, lusting, lost, disoriented. I'm a jumbled lump, maimed or mutilated.

Maybe not.

In radical and cataclysmic change I am re-forming through seeming deformation. I am dramatically altering the fiction of my life. Accidents of growth, which are the volcanics of the unconscious, cause transformation.

Russell writes to me,

I am more than you ever dreamed . . .

You will never be safe.[30]

Life can be more unpredictable than dreams, and love, just as the psychic quest of artist and critic, of blood sisters and blood brothers, is never safe.

Notes

"Jeez Louise" has been delivered at:
Louise Bourgeois colloquium in conjunction with Louise Bourgeois exhibition, Washington University, St. Louis, Missouri, October 1988
ARC Gallery, Chicago, Illinois, November 1988
Centenary College, Shreveport, Louisiana, October 1989
Brigham Young University, Provo, Utah, November 1990

1. Ruth Meyer, "Introduction," in *Louise Bourgeois,* exhibition catalogue (Cincinnati: Taft Museum, 1987), unpaginated.
2. Stuart Morgan, "Nature Study," in *Louise Bourgeois,* exhibition catalogue (Cincinnati: Taft Museum, 1987), unpaginated.
3. Ibid.
4. Ibid.
5. William Rubin, "Foreword," in Deborah Wye, *Louise Bourgeois,* exhibition catalogue (New York: Museum of Modern Art, 1982), 11.

6. Deborah Wye, "Louise Bourgeois: 'One and Others,'" in Deborah Wye, *Louise Bourgeois*, exhibition catalogue (New York: Museum of Modern Art, 1982), 13.
7. Ibid., 29.
8. Ibid., 33.
9. Louise Bourgeois, quoted in Wye, "Louise Bourgeois," 67.
10. Russell Dudley, letters to Joanna Frueh, 1988.
11. I play with the Troggs's "Wild Thing," *Wild Thing*, Atco 33193.
12. Arlene Raven, "h a r m o n i e s: Harmony Hammond," in Arlene Raven, *Crossing Over: Feminism and Art of Social Change* (Ann Arbor: UMI, 1988), 33. Originally "h a r m o n i e s," pamphlet (Chicago: Klein Gallery, 1982).
13. Dudley, letters.
14. Donald Kuspit, "Louise Bourgeois: Where Angels Fear to Tread," *Artforum* 25 (March 1987): 119.
15. Louise Bourgeois, quoted in Wye, "Louise Bourgeois," 75.
16. Endpapers by Louise Bourgeois, in *Louise Bourgeois* (New York: Bellport, 1986).
17. Morgan, "Nature Study," unpaginated.
18. Dudley, letters.
19. Louise Bourgeois, quoted in Wye, "Louise Bourgeois," 25.
20. Robert Storr, "Louise Bourgeois: Gender and Possession," *Art in America* 71 (April 1983): 135.
21. Louise Bourgeois, quoted in Lucy R. Lippard, "Louise Bourgeois: From the Inside Out," *Artforum* 13 (March 1975): 31.
22. Dudley, letters.
23. Wye, "Louise Bourgeois," 33.
24. Louise Bourgeois, quoted in Wye, "Louise Bourgeois," 95.
25. Ibid., 72.
26. Stuart Morgan, "Lair," in *Louise Bourgeois*, exhibition catalogue (Cincinnati: Taft Museum, 1987), unpaginated.
27. Dante Gabriel Rossetti, "The Woodspurge," in Jerome H. Buckley, ed., *The Pre-Raphaelites* (New York: Modern Library, 1968), 67.
28. Ibid.
29. Jerry Gorovoy, "Louise Bourgeois and the Nature of Abstraction," in *Louise Bourgeois* (New York: Bellport, 1986), unpaginated.
30. Dudley, letters.

PYTHIA

[A long table with a gavel on it sits center stage and separates two music stands, each one holding a copy of the script. Frueh enters stage right and stops at the music stand nearest to her. A hip-high stool waits by the stage-left music stand. Stage right is dark and shadowy, like a cave. Stage left is warm, golden. Frueh stands when she is at stage right and sits stage left. A shawl of gold beads and sequins covers Frueh's shoulders and breasts. A deep red-brown velvet skirt bares her navel and hangs to the floor. Her feet are bare. Frueh stands very straight, places her hands on the music stand, and speaks as if she is simultaneously telling a secret and giving a proclamation.]

Listen. Nobody likes you. Not even the one you call wife. You come to me for counsel, climb the mountain, slow, breathless, dazed by exertion. Were your feet bare like mine, they would be bleeding. Me, I wear my blood on my mouth. True red. It is not a simple color.

You desire deliverance and yearn for promises that are predictions of love coming your way, so you expect others to redeem you. You think you are a saint, but you play the role of a seeker. Any saint would tell you: the seeker does not play a role, the seeker is a lover.

You, a walking confession, are stuck on your sincerity, which you confuse with integrity. Sincerity means only that outward appearance and actual character match. That definition includes neither grace nor soundness. Sincerity is the liar's path. Look at yourself. You avert your eyes. You protect your aversion to truth, your belligerent ignorance. I hear you saying, under your breath, "I am the lover, the shy lover." You are always convincing yourself: my children love me, I am amiable, easy, and everyone is difficult, intractable, so they, like pigs and fishes, cannot be persuaded, I am a star rising from the muck of women and men. You speak about pigs and fishes the way you speak about assholes: you denigrate the animals and the body. Observe my hands and shoulders: no wings, no wand. I am not a mountain goddess, a dream to which ziggurats were built, a deity, inarticulate to every passing present, who mixes with a long-gone pantheon of stars. I told every single star just how bleak I think you are, and now I'm telling you, and I am gleaming.

The walking confession betrays his unconvincing authority. The only gaits you know are graceless: belly out, shoulders up, neck compressed, legs weak from the weight of sincerity.

[*Frueh's voice is dulcet and seductive.*]
Hummingbird, sucker, you try to extract nectar from my breath, which you feel hot, almost dripping, on your face. My mild voice and its melodious touch you mistake for a caress, but intimacy is not a condition of my love. You are desperate for a fortune cookie as you watch my lips shape your life. And you begin to know that your voice resonates in the wrong places, not in your pelvis, diaphragm, or the length of your legs, not from the top of your head or the heart of your mouth. You are ready to screech or cry, for sincerity is no substitute for grace.

So come in closer, further, to the lap, the lips, my medicinal blood.

Tiny scarlet flowers in the desert produce large, vibrant scents.

Think about the red words: grace and eros.

Remember once you leave my voice that the mountain is a place of orientation and that you came to get your bearings.

Then remember that what I say is fact and fiction, and all of it is true.

[*Table. Frueh sings.*]

Like a bird on a wire
Like a drunk in a midnight choir
I have tried in my way to be free[1]

• • •

[*Sitting.*]

A meeting with the Pythia required a snaking climb up Mount Parnassus to Delphi. Pythia was also Pythoness, a name derived from Python, who guarded the oracle, which was Pythia's location, words, and person. Python was the Greek *drakōn*, which means serpent, dragon, literally the seeing one.

[*Frueh's voice is commanding, nasty, and charming.*]

Python, my graceful tongue to crush loudmouthed visitors. We see them under the whitehot sun. They feel heavy and thirsty, and they are starving for advice. They are tearful and can barely breathe, and they wonder if the light and air will kill them before they are brought to me to ask one question. I am your dragon lady, full of word-honey, wind me round with the love I owe them. They are puking on the temple and sanctuary stones, ready for this comfortable cave. Underground we wrestle with volcanoes.

Visitors described the oracle at Delphi as cleft, gorge, and chasm. They talked about a precipice, the dark mountainside, hairpin turns, and the hot and heavy air, like a dragon's breath, they said. Pythia sat or stood before the people who came for her command, prediction, warning, prohibition, or approval, and they claimed, after hiking, fasting, praying, and ascending the steep flight of steps that led to Pythia, singer of Delphi, once called Pytho after the graceful tongue, that dragon's breath rose from the deep fissure at her feet. No one except a Pythia knew how deep that crevice was. Visitors simply said they saw and smelled its stinking vapors that supposedly sent her into trance or madness or simply made her ill, so that she had to vomit her words.

From Pythia's clefts and orifices a perfume floated when she spoke, and it was sweeter than a first-time lover's intentions. Some scholars say the scent was concentrated at her navel, so visitors would stare at it. They felt safer looking there than into her eyes. In the same way that Delphi exerted a downward pull on the body, as if forcing someone to draw closer to the earth, Pythia attracted her questioner. This effect, called Eros's Invitation, at once soothed and terrified visitors, whose preparation for the meeting entailed many repetitions of one of her maxims: the lover is a seeker who becomes sought after.

. . .

I, Dragon Lady, am, like Delphi, the site of erotic intersections. The navel is the center of the body, and Delphi, called Navel of the World, is one of the earth's geographical centers. The builders knew this, for they founded Pytho at the junction of two major dragon lines. That crossing causes dry mouth, vertigo, tears, hard breathing, heaviness, and earthward attraction. Enjoy with me the subterranean encounters of arm to shoulder, hip to pelvis, cunt to anus, back to buttocks, breasts to ribs to belly, head to neck to chin to jaw moving as my mouth moves ready for a mouth like yours, like loam, on thigh to knee to ankle, then on the feet, which, simply by walking, are intimate with the ground. Together we are at the center and see dragon lines, currents that connect one navel to another, whether it be oracular site of earth or body. Delphi to Chartres to Borobodur to Chaco to Teotihuacán; chest to chest, calf over buttocks, tongue on finger, head on stomach: they are the same, for all centers, all points and moments of concentration, are erotic.

I weed dandelions for hours and see their centers when I close my eyes at night.

Pythia, they say you hypnotize yourself in order to let go of everyday distractions.

One word in a book occupies me for days.

They say you chew laurel leaves, which take you into poetic and erotic frenzy.

Between sets of lat pulldowns I sit in the gym, staring seemingly at nothing, and a voice next to me intrudes: "Wake up. Get back to work."

The inattentive observer mistakes concentration for absentmindedness.

The second day of my period we are fucking and afterwards my blood mesmerizes my lover. Russell calls what he sees, what I feel on my thighs, buttocks, and lower back, a hemorrhage, and when I stand up, blood from my vagina and the sheets runs down my legs and drips on the floor. Russell tells me later that *hemorrhage* is an inadequate word, unequal to his perception. "Gallons, through the sheets, through the bed, through the floor," he says. The Dogon say that "a woman without adornment is speechless." I say that style is in the body, its size, movements, and spirit, rich colors are often reds, and decoration is information. The different colors of menstrual red flow from my hips: raisin, crimson, muddy mucus. All the better to kiss you with.

Pythia, they say you wear white, to speak your virginity. I see a picture of you painted by a nineteenth-century artist, and you are wearing red and umber. You are barefoot and your skirt touches the ground, where a snake that is far too small rests next to a smoking fissure. In another nineteenth-century painting I see you with your breasts bare and a huge python emerging from between your thighs. Virgin, for you, means "my choice," and your questioners never think that Pytho is either only a spectacular phallus that you need as your companion or an external vagina that represents the origin of your counsels. Only a fool speaks from her cunt alone.

They say that oracular voice necessitates madness. But no one listens to women called mad. No one listened to Cassandra. History has reduced her to less than tears. A synopsis of the Trojan War doesn't mention her once. One scholar says that cultural myth grants seers such as Cassandra the dubious privilege of speaking from the simultaneously despised and romanticized lower mouth. You see, but visions do not possess you. Sometimes you speak in the precision of riddles, more often in the considered words of the learned woman you are. Speaking only from the cunt would make any woman mad.

[*Frueh shifts position more consciously than she has yet done in this section.*]

In graduate school my professor wore a red velvet suit. He was impersonating the menstrual female, though he would never have thought that. He liked to think of himself as a nineteenth-century dandy. He wore socks when we fucked, and they signaled his inhibition. All along he rejected my seduction, which he thought was madness. One day I said to him, "I think I know what it would feel like to be crazy." He said, "Sometimes I see madness in your eyes." I hadn't asked for confirmation, but I was in danger, for the bloodman's words cut, they felt as real as prophecy. Too easily I equated prophecy with apocalypse.

Many years later a friend said to me, "Your mind is like a diamond."

"What do you mean?" I asked.

"Hard and sharp," she answered.

This new insight conferred sanity. Until then I had feared sanity as a lukewarm hell of normalcy. My friend disagreed. "Sanity isn't about the status quo," she said.

[*Table. Frueh taps the gavel gracefully, as if calling a group to order. Subsequent use of the gavel is the same.*]

Test the law.

[*Standing.*]

You believe in one-to-one correspondences.

I saw red hair on an ancient woman. I saw a man turning into a wolf. I saw the skyscrapers start to walk.

Appearances fool you into belief. Let your senses lead you into existence as a totality of ensembles, all present together, in series of manifestation and obscurity.

The mother's and daughter's voices sound the same over the telephone.

Dying lilacs in a vase smell like urine drying on a toilet bowl.

I taste like salt and smell like a rose.

The Romance of the Rose is a medieval narrative that smells of sex, and the Harlequin romance is a rosy story, for players win the often losing game of love in the Western world. The tales of Tristan and Iseult, Romeo and Juliet, and Thomas à Becket and Henry II are three of myriad love songs whose fixation on love indicates its absence in practice.

The half-full cup is half empty. Either way, grief overruns the empty heart.

Gold flows from the graceful tongue, and silence is golden, too. Maybe you do not hear my words, for speech is the most easily misinterpreted of human behaviors.

[*Table. Frueh sings to the tune of "White Coral Bells."*]

Red coral bells upon a slender stalk

Bleeding hearts and roses deck my garden walk

O, don't you wish that you could hear them ring

That will happen only when the prophets sing

[*Sitting.*]

I walk home where there are no sidewalks. Often I see nails on the street, usually near a curb. I used to pick them up, but I don't anymore.

Ruthless compassion takes root in the good Samaritan's heart. Conditions replace one another so that good and evil may not be easily distinguishable and one can become the other. (Move fast the way Satan and the angels do.) Evil derives from the Indo-European *upo,* up from under. Evil moves into view and scales the human body to reach heaven.

My friend Edith says, "You know how to move. See how you pack one suitcase fast so you can go anywhere."

Pythia, chew your laurel, so the ecstasy of enigmatic speech, province of the poet, the lover, and the prophet, will speed the movement of your mind over matter, like a goat up Mount Parnassus. Your listeners, not you, are in a trance.

My mother-in-law says, "So you're a Capricorn. Tell me about Capricorn."

"Sign of the goat," I say. "Observe my horns, my hooves."

Russell saw them the first time he looked at me, even though I wore red boots and my horns didn't glow then, in daylight, as much as they do in darkness. Like the time we were sitting in the living room and I was watching his white T-shirt, the white tapers on the table, and the white roses floating in a bowl between the candlesticks as I tried to observe the exact advent of night.

In the little forest outside my parents' living room it seemed like sundown all day. The sky was overcast and the trees were exceptionally lush from an unusually rainy spring. Mom and Dad called the forest "our jungle" that summer a couple of years ago. They had a fight during which Dad got sullen and Mom got frustrated. Afterwards she felt that she had been too harsh on him, and a slamming door convinced her that Dad had left the house. She sent me looking for him. I walked into the forest. Dad wasn't sitting on any of the benches he'd placed on the path. I saw bones and birds, and I expected to see Dad's corpse laying in the compost or around a curve. Animals stirred, but quiet overwhelmed me. In quiet times, anything can happen. What goes up need not come down. Gravity is not the only consequence of grace. Cock up, cock down; body grows tall, body gets buried; facelift, ten-years-after sag. Denials of gravity are temporary, for grace overrides gravity. Grace is not higher than me, higher than you, as rarefied as gods of light, like Apollo, who took over the Delphic Oracle by killing Python. Some say Apollo also killed Delphyne, the Pythia at that time, by slitting her throat. He had to see her blood, which he called "dark and demented," and then his blade—such an earthly weapon—disappeared. No evidence. Delphyne, delirium, delphinium, which is sometimes poisonous. Delphyne, only toxic to the gods who say light is an absolute. After Delphyne, for a length of time unknown to us, the Pythias were teenagers, permitted to bear children, who called themselves brides and wives of Apollo. (Take me, O my god of consummate light, for I am dressed in a pale desire, like Mary's lilies in the radiance of a later god.) One young Pythia was abducted, and from then on the oracle was at least beginning menopause and usually well beyond her reproductive years. (Consort or companion of Apollo, my ass. My choice. Listen, rapist, lustrous with the glamor of high gods and angels, gold comes from the earth. Gold comes up from under.)

Grace does not derive from words meaning good or evil. The Indo-European base *gwer* means "to lift up the voice," and the Sanskrit *gṛṇāti* means "he sings."

In my parents' forest, looking for my father, I wanted to sing, even though, or because, I was full of fear. Mom and I soon discovered that Dad was in their bedroom taking a nap. In the summer when the temperature is comfortable and the windows are open upstairs, the bedroom doors, even if gently tapped to close, swing shut hard and unpredictably. I went to the study for a nap of my own, and as I fell asleep I heard, in my mind, I'm sure, my father singing:

[*Frueh sings to the tune of the traditional song, "The Demon Lover."*]

Hello, hello, my own true love
Hello, hello, cried he
I have just returned from the dark scented wood
All for the love of thee

I could have married the Angel of Death
She would have married me
But I refused her strange perfumes
All for the sake of thee

Often I am sitting at my desk when the late afternoon wind rises in summertime. Across the street the willows' limbs sway, then shake. I feel my naked arm, which is smooth and satisfying. Instantaneous voluptuousness comes over me, and Pythia calls that state singing. Sometimes she sings to her visitors.

I danced and sang with a bird watching. I had fallen in love with Russell and was getting a divorce. I felt crazy that night. First I whirled around the big living room whose curtainless windows reflected my image, and I could also see the lights of the city. I played a tape, over and over, of a dumb and passionate popular song, one of the few hits at the time that made me want to move. I turned the music off and looked at the bird. A song whose tune was as dark and melancholy as an English folksong about love and murder came out of me, but the song was about the bird. Unlike a folksong, the melody was unrepeated and rambling. The lyrics praised the bird—her sheen, her sharp eyes, her voice and movements, which I wanted to understand. (Goats dance through darkness.)

Lascivious Pythia, they say an old goat is a lecherous man. They forget your lust. Today Hormone Replacement Therapy means sex, and so does I fell into a burning ring of fire and fever, you give me fever, and the illustrations on romance book covers in the grocery store.[2] I don't see you, Pythia, on them. I see a man and a woman in their twenties. His muscles bulge. Her breasts bulge. She has long hair, and his upper body is naked. Often her skirt is hiked up to reveal her leg, bare from foot to thigh. Here we see clichés of skin to skin, which try to show what lies underneath them: it is the heart as the love muscle that strains to break free from the confinement of skin as contour. Deeper yet runs the representation of the heart's athleticism and youthful vigor: the heart has endurance and probably acrobatic skill. The cover pictures keep me at a distance, within the confines of voyeurism. I would like to observe eros and see the body as permeable, as a site of events—orgasm, toothache, sneeze, the appearance of a pimple, lesion, wart, or wrinkle—and as a condition of processes, which are the changes that lead to the events. The heart is an ancient organ, ancient like ferns, and I would like to observe the eros of ferns.

The book titles read:

[*Frueh recites the words lovingly, as if the titles were something other than dreck. Yet a hint of sarcasm colors the recitation.*]

Silver Fire, Stardust Dreams, Angel Eves, Touch Me with Fire, Forever His, Halfway to Paradise, Rebel Wind, No Other Love, The Passionate Rebel, So Wild My Heart, My Only Desire, Love's Timeless Dance, The Rogue and the Lily, The Panther and the Rose, Tender Deception, Emerald Dreams, Moon of Desire, All the Time We Need, Fascination, Wildcat, Scarlet Lady.

The asinine parody of eros that I see and read in the grocery store is a melancholy reminder of people's everyday and necessary desire for the poet's, the lover's, and the prophet's ecstasies of enigmatic speech, which is the desire for wild grace.

I am the scarlet woman
The bottomless blue lake.

[*Table. Frueh taps the gavel.*]

Scorch the law.

[*Standing.*]

Road to ruin I heard them say
The name of a bar on an old highway
See the neon burning red
In the desert of the dead
[*Table. Frueh taps the gavel.*]
Learn the law.
[*Sitting.*]

When Pythia chooses to answer, she does it clearly. When she suspects slyness in a question, she is more subtle and poetic. Sometimes a visitor, having received an answer, goes back to tell Pythia she has been vague. Pythia then says, "You heard me." Occasionally she adds, "She sells seashells by the seashore," or "Loothe lipth lithp legendth."

Pythia's first maxim, "Know thyself," later used by Socrates, was carved on the temple at Delphi. The oracle and the poet coax meaning from the seeker. They stamp out rumor and create it. "Rumors create legends," says Pythia.

Based on the few extant documents about the ancient Pythias—who practiced from before 2300 B.C. to A.D. 529, when the Roman emperor Justinian closed the schools in Greece, thereby abolishing the education of women, which meant the closing of the oracle at Delphi—scholars have reconstructed a rare public address given by the Pythia Xenocleia. Shortly before 900 B.C., she ordered the Twelve Labors of Heracles and later commanded that he be burned. She, like other Pythias, sentenced Apollo's heroes to death whenever she could in response to the heroes' string of moral and physical murders.

Scholars say that Xenocleia delivered her address in the same manner that she answered individuals, and that her manner was characteristic of Pythias: she was almost motionless, and her maintenance of a peaceful dignity made her speech measured. "She weighed her words," writes one scholar, and another reveals, in strangely unacademic prose, "I wish her beautiful voice could have excruciated me."

Here are Xenocleia's words:

Speaking is believing. My words create and eliminate. Veiling and unveiling, my voice hums in the heart, transforming the time we are together.

There is no purely physical inflection of a voice. Sounds are carriers of memory and of sensory experience, and sounds are immediate. My sounds are in you now, my body has become yours. We are breathing, all enveloped in our human breath. Inhaling and exhaling the air, the subtlety of pheromones, exchanging the denseness of hormonal rhythms, we are one breath, one body. We cross the fragmented, the manifest, and the explicit with the inseparable, the transitory, and the implicit. Sounds, like breaths and melodies, are contingencies of present, past, and future, which my sounds actively transform.

Words don't like being alone. They thrive in company. That is why tones are needed now, a song with many grace notes. My melodies transmute thought into sound and action, and, like myths and folksongs, my melodies are never fixed. Musical thinking is thinking in motions, and clear movement, like clear thinking, is erotic concentration. In the Ayurvedic *Book of Timeless Medicine,* we learn that love agrees with music, justice agrees with rites. The law, the rites, promote stagnation, for they are ascetic, like a melody with no grace notes. Dictionaries tell you that grace notes are unnecessary to the melody, but champagne has no charm without bubbles, and chocolate bars are worthless without sugar.

Grace is sweet in and of itself, the singer must not force the song. Singing with feeling inhibits fluency, for then melodrama becomes the primary inflection.

Ascetic thinking separates people from one another, as the law does, too, in contrast to love. Erotic thinking, which is dependent on melody, alleviates the loneliness of words. Melodies are dragon lines, moving to center after center of meaning. The law of light and of risen and rising angels restricts what any of us can say. What we cannot say we can sing about. So song enhances living as grace notes enhance melody. Do not misunderstand enhancement as ornamentation, the way dictionaries misrepresent the grace note as embellishment. Enhancement is necessary, for it heightens awareness.

I am aware of you listening and observing. Some of you have come to me with questions, and others of you will. Some of you have heard that my words are the law. Lawyers advise, and so do I sometimes, but they arrange sounds pleasingly in sequence in order to win, and their interest in gold is different from mine.

In this golden hour my voice grows. I fly united with the golden eagle, yellow bird, and gold-winged woodpecker. My voice moves back and forth through centuries. I last forever, for no time at all. Kiss me, my golden tongue is melting in the heat of my mouth.

[*Standing. Frueh catches the eye of a young woman in the audience for the first several lines, someone in her twenties, and looks at her pointedly off and on throughout this section.*]

You ask, "Where is home?"

It is not anywhere you think it is. Not in the library in your parents' home, not in the kitchen where you cook with friends, not with the men and women you call lover, not with your suicidal visions.

You sat on a boulder, feet in the Aegean Sea. Hours later you felt for calluses that the water had washed away. You stood on the boulder, ready to dive underwater and breathe like a mermaid.

You see everyday occurrences as possibilities of death: hair blowing across your forehead turns into a knife, slices your skin, and penetrates your cranium; a car thirty feet away speeds up and rams into your car head on; honeysuckle petals become plutonium pellets that force themselves into your mouth and down your throat.

Road signs scare you: Watch for Rocks; Runaway Truck; Hitchhikers May Be Inmates; Truckers, Check Brakes; Rattlesnakes; Exit Now.

You're afraid that because things have gone to hell, they'll probably stay there.

You're wondering if you should keep turning the other cheek.

Release your pain, and you'll relax. Prepare for another slap, and call self-sacrifice victimhood.

Your enemies have given you more strength than they can even imagine for themselves. You will change history as we know it.

Decisions of magnitude do not require time. Consideration is only a leap of faith to a path as true as the next one when the traveler has begun another journey.

Repeat my next words after you have left me:

I am a *fauve*
True to my kind
I am a *fauve*
And we're all divine
I am a *fauve*
An experiment in terror
I am a *fauve*
A formidable error

I tell you to recite these lines, very soon now and also before you go to sleep tonight, because you call yourself an ugly animal. As the dancer

Sarah of Alabama says, "Animals have beautiful bodies till they are tamed." Rapunzel, Rapunzel, let down your hair. Slouching is obedience to shame.

Make your voice more like music, and your posture will change. Your voice will help your hands, which you wring and pick at, to throw caution to the wind. Then they can begin to collect blood from broken bodies.

You know Pythia's maxims, for all questioners learn them before facing me. I choose one especially for you: do not turn back while on a journey.

Rapunzel, Rapunzel, let down your hair, for you must sing a song. Sweetie, I will brush your hair as you are singing.

[*Frueh sings to any tune that comes to her mind.*]

Wild as a nun running to god
Wild as a runner unaware of the weather
Wild as a player who's forgotten the game
Wild is the crooner who knows your real name

[*Sitting. Frueh continues to sing.*]

Wild the stargazer who knows when to stop
Wild the weightlifter who lightens her load
Wild laughing singer who coughs up her aria
Wild is the wanderer on a new road

Pythia wanders into a rigorous initiation. Initiation is the death of old ways. Study and revelation are the methods she learns, and they establish eros in body and mind. The disciplines of reading and dreaming day and night, of moving mind and body, one's own and others', creates Pythia, who, according to ancient and contemporary scholars, is hardheaded and amorous. She learns to read people, fields of energy and fields of wheat, not only books. She dreams in the lake, in the gym, on the toilet, and in her lovers' eyes.

She disobeys injunctions against knowledge, for the severest education forces the initiate to reject the law. This rejection cannot be rebellion, for then the would-be Pythia fails. In order to complete her initiation she must demonstrate her understanding and rejection of the law. Below are some successful examples of this task, recorded by the Pythias' archivists, preserved in the oracular cave, and discovered only five years ago and published in a slender volume.

The Pythia Daphne says:

The law came to my door

Armed with a gavel and gun
It said, I'll blow your head off
Or beat you down for fun
I said, law, you are a mother
And you're a father, too
But I am not your daughter, law,
And you don't have a clue

The Pythia Peggy says, in honor of Daphne's first line:

The law came to my door, or was it a traveling salesman dressed in the rags of a guy named Christ who needed a better tailor? I remember now, he wore an Armani suit. I wear one myself for some clients. I butter their bread on both sides so that they can't avoid grease spots.

The Pythia Themistoclea says:

The law is a laboring woman
The law is a retching man.

The Pythia Helen says:

Law, you are the bastard who believes that love has died.

The Pythia Edith says:

Silence is golden. Speech is golden. I hear golden rule after golden rule: blessed be the lawyers, for they are great; hail, false prophets, for they are great; hail, executioner, for you are grace.

The Pythia Renée says:

Bring on the apocalypse
Give us the holocaust, too
Shit on every advocate
Of what we call virtue
Now I hear the moralists
Who stand on such high ground
That they all call it heaven
When the rest of us aren't around.

Pythia, let me tell you a story you may not have heard. The time is the Inquisition.

> Perhaps surprisingly, given their heinousness, the tactics of the inquisitors were closely regulated. Lawyers were required to remain at the side of heretics and to note every word they said as they were tortured; lawyers also recorded how long the torture lasted and what specific methods were used. The law was explicit that a person could not be tortured more than once unless new evidence came to light, but

> torturers could use whatever method they felt suitable to the case—deprivation of sleep, use of the rack, or a water torture in which the victims feared they would suffocate. When the victim was given a chance to confess, a lawyer would record willingness or reluctance. In the name of the law it was possible to carry out the most hideous practices.[3]

[*Frueh picks up the gavel and throws it upstage. Standing.*]

You are an abomination. Yet you come here asking, "What does it mean to be a saint?" Sit tight. Do not bat an eye. Heaven's thread is thin, like a filament of mucus from your nose. Life hangs by a noose, and you deserve death songs.

You say, "Life is precious," "God is merciful," "Do good unto others and they will do good unto you," and "I would do anything for love." Sing a song of menace for a pocketful of lies. I'll sew your heart right onto your sleeve. Ten buckets of disinfectant and four months of constant sunlight cannot clean your closet, thick with dung and mildew. Liar, liar, pants on fire. Your nose is stuck in a wild rose briar.

A saint has dignity. When you perform hysterectomies and Caesarean sections, you say, "I'll give the pretty women an almost invisible scar, but the ugly women, what have they got to preserve? so I'll leave them with a gash, with flesh that heals in the form of a tattered fabric." You think that you're keeping beauty and ugliness where they belong. All acts of maintenance are attempts to achieve grace. But acts of grace do not support the status quo, for Eros is an outlaw who demands the proliferation of polymorphous perversities. You enforce conformity to aesthetic standards, for you cannot believe that any woman not beautiful in your eyes could be sexual, since you wouldn't want to fuck her. You see women's lust as a treatable condition: fuck a woman, or wreck her. These treatments are the same, for they both inflict limitation. The human option for polymorphous perversities means that people can desire difference: Saint Joan wears men's clothes; Saint Onuphrius, alone in the desert for sixty years, dresses himself in a garland of oleander petals and winds his own long hair around the flowers; Saint Arlene attaches her dead raven companion to the belt at her waist and lets the bird rot and shrivel there; Saint Gargantua eats beyond his heart's desire and weighs a quarter of a ton; Saint Rachel, at age fifty, shaves her head and wears fuschia lipstick. You tell your colleagues that your surgeries are fastidious assessments of beauty, but the saints, in their excesses of ordinary desire, are far more fastidious than you. For a saint, your sense of aesthetics is a shrunken vision. You are like the fifteenth-century monks of many orders who, in one huge volume filled with all their imaginings about women, write, "The root of evil is carnal greed, with which the female sex befouls itself at birth."

Pythias Phemonoë, Daphne, Peggy, Claire, Themistoclea, Helen, Manto, Edith, and Renée say, "We have an appetite. Cock Robin, we are lascivious and insatiable."

Merle, French for blackbird, will fly, right over you, right over to you, cover your eyeballs with a wing. Wing will grow and blind you with its beauty. Wing will be a black shadow on your heart. Shadow will cool your cock, flap, and banish your desire. Wing will be as big as the sun.

My voice is the beginning of your requiem. Hear the other instruments approaching: whistle, reed flute, electric guitar, violin, castanets, dulcimer, tabor, tambourine. Someone says, "Robin, cock robin, robin redbreast, robin's egg blue, robbin' you blind, robber baron, rubber penis, rub yourself raw, Robin, Cock Robin, diminutive of Robert, bright in fame, the lightning rod, the little robber, darling robber, the lovely thief."

[*Frueh sings.*]

Who killed Cock Robin?
Who killed Cock Robin?
I, said the sparrow,
With my little bow and arrow
It was I, O, it was I
Who killed Cock Robin?
Who killed Cock Robin?
Me, I'll be blunt,
With my bloody cunt
It was I, O, it was I

[*Table. Frueh sings. Her voice is sometimes honeyed, sometimes mean and she snarls.*]

I see your true colors shining through
I see your true colors in all you do
So don't be afraid to let them show[4]

[*Sitting. Articulated with exceptional clarity and deliberateness.*]

Kaylee ojin. Quasit jilian. Ansee jasha curarania. Hwang ma shacka coumarine, tay sue sotue rangingba. Fot wojan keer, sarter olipoge, eeg fot dimiastique, fectique, romoussin. Caw, caw, anzhi dang deam cway. Eert, mofsnickenforoot. Dao orte sute ortée maglophorion.

[*Standing. Frueh looks at an old(er) woman in the audience and continues, now and then, to address her.*]

You feel like a monster. Then maybe you can be a saint. You are ashamed of your appetite. Remember the meals you've shared with your girlfriends, the ones you've cooked together and the ones enjoyed in restaurants. Remember the bottles of wine, the pastas, crèmes caramels, breads, sweet butter, eggs Benedict, moules marinières, peaches, coffee, sausage, tender chicken, honey, salad greens, shrimp, chocolate. Remember Cabernet, Merlot, Pinot Noir, the reds you've lingered over with your girlfriends and other lovers. Remember masturbating forcefully, deliberately when you were a girl. Once your mother saw you, in your nylon nightgown, sitting on her piano bench, pressing your legs together so that near the pelvic joint the tops of your inner thighs would press your labia to your clitoris. You knew, at eight, the use of subtle pressures. Sometimes they make you come when you don't expect to, in your sleep—and you wake up pressing harder—while reading in a chair—and you keep your legs crossed for minutes at the angle that began the orgasm, which continues as long as you don't move your legs.

In your younger days you listened to a lot of lyrics in which pride is always foolish and rhymes with hide.

Shaking/quaking
Yearning/burning/tossing and turning
Lightning/frightening
Right/tonight
Street/meet
You/I do
Desire/fire/higher
Mine/all the time.

You hear Elvis whining, "I don't want no other love. Baby, it's still you I'm thinking of."[5] Love is cruel to the fool.

"Just stop breaking my heart," you say. "I'm tired of falling into the arms of strangers. My earrings always get in the way when I kiss, and my hair gets stuck in my teeth, because I'm the pussy whirlpool, always testing the waters of my lust, testing my patience, too."

You say,
"Conclude/rude

"Sex/perplex

"Use/re-fuse:

"Or is it ref-use?"

You say,

"Empress Messalina challenged a prostitute to a contest. Who, the whore or Messalina, could fuck more men in a night? Messalina won, and her husband, Claudius, had her beheaded."

You say,

"Roman Empress took men on in a game of win and lose
Lost her head, not simply pride. Bad girls get abused.

"Bad and good and lose and win, I can't tell which is which
The Messalina in me says, I'll fuck you, I'm a bitch."

You say,

"I want to screw you, feel your cock screwing into me, feel your hips unscrewing my lust, screw you flush to the fucking bed. We will be screwed up, together, in my internal, eternal thread, spiralled into our thick cunt, screwing around, and around and around in the revolutions, the evolution of grace."

You say,

"Amused/confused

"Do I put on my Bible belt, my garter belt, the cinch of prophecy, my chastity belt, my menstrual pad? Do I pull out my tampon for the last time? That bloody plug is my last remnant of a trashcan love, your sterilization of scarlet. Good golly, Miss Molly, I am a storm and a half of eros, a hurricane of vicissitudes."[6]

I say,

Lust/must

Appetite/bite

The root of *proud* is a Latin word meaning to be useful. Benefit yourself. Monster, you are more than a warning to conditional femininity, whose doctrine is cleanliness: wear this sea mud, honey, clay, and mummy mask; wipe that blood from your mouth; shave those wildebeest legs; we want cologne between your thighs. Monster, how clean do you think you need to be for grace? You are ready to extinguish the femininity that requires you to wash and scent yourself until you smell like some moron's dream of Cleopatra. Monster, you are femininity to the *n*th degree. Out of bounds, off-limits, living among the unsuspecting, at their very side, you are the woman of my dreams.

[*Table. Frueh sings.*]

> Amazing grace, how sweet the sound
> That changed someone like me
> I once was lost but now am found
> Was blind but now I see

[*Sitting.*]

When Apollo killed Python, an act intended to conquer Pythia, he used a thousand arrows, which Renaissance mythographers equated with sun rays.

(The name of my lipstick *is* True Red.)

One source says Apollo planned to conquer Pythia because he wanted the oracle to be for men only. He said, "Men, more than women, need to learn gentility and self-control."[7] Those were the words of a subtle politician who tried to suppress the extremity of Pythia's femininity. She saw many men. Odysseus, Plato, Plutarch, Agamemnon, Croesus, Laius and his son Oedipus visited her. So did Pythagoras, and Pythia was his teacher as well as the oracle who answered him. Pythia saw Socrates, too, and he took her first maxim, "Know thyself."

(I want to fuck them all. Fuck 'em all.)

Pythia saw women whenever she wanted to, although Apollo's attitude ushered in an era, not dead yet, in which many people do not know the difference between a vagina and a vulva. Nor can they pronounce clit′-or-is correctly.

(I am on slow boil, in continuous heat. Pythia foretold the eruption of Vesuvius.)

In my gym a plexiglas sign hanging overhead reads, Sin blinds men's eyes / Grace opens them.

Because Eros symbolizes the darkness associated with sin, he is represented blindfolded in much art. One of the lesser gods in Greek mythology, Eros is blindfolded also because, we are told, love is blind. How easy it is to abandon eros for fear of falling—in love and into the arms of strangers, those exotics who crave far more than the body.

("I've buried Python's body," says Pythia to Apollo, "and you, blinded by the light, will never find my Python.")

We neither fall nor rise in love. We undulate and spiral in consuming exoticism, the strange ways of grace.

A young man comes to my house to take me to the airport. He waits while I put on my jacket and gloves. I see him stare, I know attraction when I see it. He is about to speak, to say something as simple as, "You look great," but he remains silent.

Jocasta is more interesting than her son Oedipus. My young friend feared the power of mother over son, and I can't fault him for that, yet every old(er) woman is not Jocasta waiting for a loving Oedipus who will fuck her, then rip his eyes out because he can no longer bear seeing her beauty and feeling more than her body. The Freudian story of the castrated woman is a keystone in the dread of old(er) women, and so is Freud's story of the self-blinded man. The old(er) body is shrinking, wrinkling flesh, representative of phallic failure, and men do not want to penetrate the site of desire's death. True penetration, which is understanding, requires eyes, mind, and speech, not simply a penis.

(Pythia, you glimmer indistinctly to almost all the men Apollo wants you to see, all the men who blunder in fear when they say to themselves, "Oh, Pythia, I cannot look you in the eyes.")

I laugh at the salacious, strutting masculinity ignorant of old(er) women's lusts: "I make old women blush, I make young girls squeal." So boasts George Thorogood in "Bad to the Bone."[8] Blind to the bone. Narcissistic masculinity such as Thorogood's constructs a femininity in which old(er) women are at once scatological and syrupy sweet: the first blunder continually resuscitates the witch, who has lingered in the Western imagination from the mid-fifteenth century on as voraciously and horrifyingly, yet laughably, lustful; the second blunder posits old(er) women as pure and defeminized, unsexed once they are nonreproductive. In this configuration the scatological old(er) woman can neither understand obscenity nor participate in the erotic. This is high irony. Monsters enjoy irony, but it is also a burden.

(Monsters don't age gracefully. Aging gracefully means diminishing one's appetite. Monsters have the grace of a python crushing prey.)

[*Frueh lifts her skirt to reveal one leg from thigh to foot.*]

See me age before your eyes. The spider veins are forming webbing on my legs, another hair turned gray with the touch of my last sentence on your inner ear. I am the untapped resource of time running out. I am in a constant state of grooming, or shall I call it maintenance, even repair? I must secure myself from the patterns of movement I appear to praise. So I bodybuild, enjoy a monthly facial, eat grapenuts and nonfat yogurt, tofu and hot peppers, tuna with herbs and vinegar, and get close to drunk occasionally on champagne. Name those behaviors narcissism, self-indulgence, fitness, and the fear of flesh that moves.

Rachel writes me a letter, tells me to "take care of your gorgeous self," and I am shocked. I feel like a monster, born with too few models for my gorgeous self to avoid becoming a parody of sex and beauty, words muffled by the mystique of youth. Do I keep my hair dark, dye the references to oncoming death, blacken out the wisdom I'm afraid that people fear? I look up *gorgeous* in the dictionary. *Gorgeous* comes from the Latin *gurges*, whirlpool, throat. My beauty is sticking in my throat. The throat sucks back any words in my defense, and they swirl around and around, going nowhere, like puke that has no place to go. I am nauseous, nauseating, like the forty-five-year-old star known for her sexual glamor and body-baring dress, who says she looks ridiculous. She adds, "It's a hard job, but someone's got to do it." The ridiculous is trivial and memorable. The only way to be serious is to make a joke, gorge ourselves, the gorgeous women of fearsome sexual glamor, on our own absurdity.

Take care of your gorgeous self. I will not be a joke. A joke is an amusing trick, an exaggeration that provokes laughter or contempt, and it is inconsistent with common sense. I will be the joker, the unsuspected difficulty that lies about old women can't control. I will use oracular voice, which makes uncommon sense.

[*Frueh lets down her skirt. She takes the last page of the text. Table.*]

[*Said in a tone whose softness of breath reminds people of a whisper.*]

I am as sultry as the desert night, ninety-four degrees at two A.M. Let me take you to the saguaros. We will avoid the places people say gangsters dump dead bodies. Then let me take you, out to breakfast, lunch, and dinner, let me take your hands in mine, so I can soothe them with sweet lotion, then you can braid my hair and fuck me again. I grab the curls at the nape of your neck, and I see that your lips are wet. You are luscious, you grace my eyes, and your voice is soft like Python moving over my legs, you grace my speech, I am a serpent without venom and a bulldog for you whom I love.

Bulldog bulldike bulldagger, I re-wed you daily, I will stab my loving tongue wherever necessary to grace your name, I love your cockrush, smells, from breath to shit to underarm, your erotic agitation and agility, all your effluvia.

[*Frueh gently places the page on the table and exits stage left.*]

Notes

"Pythia" has been performed at:
Pioneer Center for the Performing Arts, Reno, Nevada, March 1994, as part of Daring Explorations Theater Company's programming
Southwest Society of Photographic Education Conference, Tucson, Arizona, October 1994

1. Leonard Cohen, "Bird on a Wire," *Songs from a Room,* Columbia CS-9767.
2. I've incorporated lyrics from Johnny Cash, "Ring of Fire," *Ring of Fire,* Columbia CS-8853, and Peggy Lee, "Fever," Capitol 3998.
3. I have altered Lawrence S. Wrightman and Saul M. Kassan, *Confessions in the Courtroom* (Newbury Park: Sage Publications, 1993), 60–61.
4. Cyndi Lauper, "True Colors," *True Colors,* Columbia 40313.
5. Elvis Presley, "Don't Be Cruel," *Elvis' Golden Records,* RCA LPM-1701.
6. I've incorporated the title of Little Richard's "Good Golly Miss Molly," *Little Richard,* Camden CAL-420.
7. Norma Lorre Goodrich, *Priestesses* (New York: Harper, 1990), 204, quotes Strabo: "My source Ephorus recounts the history of Delphi this way: Apollo conquered the Pythia because he wanted the oracle for men only, because men (more than women) need to be taught gentility and self-control."
8. George Thorogood, "Bad to the Bone," *Bad to the Bone,* EMI 17076.

Art and Photography Credits

Page 27. Russell Dudley and Joanna Frueh.
Page 28. Russell Dudley and Joanna Frueh.
Page 29. Photographer unknown.
Pages 30–33. Russell Dudley and Joanna Frueh.
Pages 34–35. Bill Hedrich, Hedrich-Blessing Studio, courtesy the Chicago Historical Society.
Page 37. Russell Dudley and Joanna Frueh.
Page 93. *Left:* Bailey Doogan, *Mass,* 1991–92, 72 inches × 48 inches, oil on canvas, righthand panel of diptych (overall size of diptych: 72 × 144). *Right:* Bailey Doogan, *Mea Corpa,* 1992, 72 inches × 48 inches, oil on canvas. Photos by Andrew Harkins. Reprinted courtesy Bailey Doogan.
Page 151. Hannah Wilke, *July 26, 1992/February 19, 1992: #4 from INTRA-VENUS,* 1992–93, 2 panels: 71 1/2 inches × 47 1/2 inches each, chromagenic supergloss prints. Photos by Dennis Cowley, courtesy Ronald Feldman Fine Arts, New York.
Page 215. Russell Dudley and Joanna Frueh.

Index

Joanna Frueh is Associate Professor of Art History at the University of Nevada, Reno, and the author of Hannah Wilke: A Retrospective *(1989).*

Designer:	Nola Burger
Compositor:	Impressions Book and Journal Services, Inc.
Text:	11/13.75 Fournier
Display:	Futura
Printer:	Edwards Brothers, Inc.
Binder:	Edwards Brothers, Inc.